DAY TRADING OPTIONS

A CRASH COURSE FOR BEGINNERS ON HOW TO INVEST IN THE STOCK MARKET, INCLUDING TECHNICAL ANALYSIS, TRADING PSYCHOLOGY, AND USEFUL STRATEGIES.

Matthew Swing

TABLE OF CONTENTS

Introduction

An option is simply a contract between two parties which is based on an underlying asset. You can create an options contract for any type of asset, but our focus is on options contracts for stocks. They are called options because one party of the contract will have the option to buy or sell stocks depending on whether or not certain conditions are met.

Learning the lingo

- **Put Option:** A put option is an option contract to sell a particular stock under the terms of the put option contract. With a put option, you are 'putting it into the ownership' of the option buyer.

- **Call Option:** A call option is a contract to buy a stock according to the terms of the call option contract. A call option means you are calling upon the seller to sell you the stock, at the contract terms.

- **Long and Short:** Call options have two subsets; long and short. When you buy a call option to open a trade, you are said to be buying a long call. When you sell a call option to close a trade, you are selling a long call. When you sell a call to open a trade, you are said to be selling a short call. When you act to close that trade, you are buying a short call. As the price of the stock rises, your call option also rises in value.

- **American Option:** An American option is an option, whether a put or a call, that can be exercised at any time before the expiration date. American options are usually sold on the stock market.

- **European Option:** A European option can only be exercised on the expiration date, not before. However, it can be sold before the expiration date. European options are generally sold on the "Over the Counter" or OTC market.

- **Buyer and Seller:** For every purchase or sale there must be a sale or purchase that corresponds with it. The table below describes that correspondence for the buyer and seller. Notice that the buyer has the option but not the obligation to act, whereas the seller has the obligation to act if the buyer chooses to execute the option. Here, we refer in the most general sense to an investment 'instrument' which could be common stock or, for example, an ETF.

- **Execute:** This means that the buyer decides to act on the contract, to buy or sell; that is to execute the contract. It is also referred to as Exercising the Option.

- **Expiration Date:** When the contract is agreed upon, it runs for some finite period of time. After the expiration date, the contract expires; that is, it's no longer valid. After the expiration date, the value of the option is zero.

- **Market Price:** Market price is the current price of that stock today. Market prices vary minute by minute on the stock exchange.

- **Option Premium:** There is a cost for buying an options contract, either put or call. That charge, collected by the seller, depends on the length of the contract and the practice of the broker. Premiums can range from a few cents per contract to closer to $20. Option premiums are paid in cash; the cash you have in your brokerage account.

- **Intrinsic Value:** Value of the premium derived from the value of the underlying stock.

- **Extrinsic Value:** Portion of the premium related to volatility and time.

Types of Options

There are primarily, only two types of options, namely the Call options and Put Options. All others are basically a combination of strategies based on the former two.

Call Option

It is an option where the underlying stock can be purchased on or before its expiration date. While purchasing a Call Option, a certain amount of premium is paid to the selling party, which gives you the right to purchase the underlying stock at a predetermined price, which is referred to as the strike price.

Put Option

It is an option where the underlying stock can be sold on or before its expiration date. It implies that you are bearish about the market and thus wishing for the underlying stock price to drop to a level which is below the strike price of the put option at which it was purchased either before or at the time of expiration.

Options Contracts

The price of the contract an individual is participating in is often determined by the type of asset being traded. The contract of an options trade is supposed to have two parties who are either buying or selling the underlying assets. Let's expound on the stock options as the underlying asset. If an individual has the potential of purchasing one hundred shares of a certain company for one hundred American dollars, this will be the determinant of the value possessed by the option contract. An underlying asset can be a market index.

The contract agreed by option trading parties is supposed to have a clear indication of which type of option is being traded. The types of options that are known in the current world tend to categorize and named depending on the varied features they pose. People across the globe are familiar with two types of options. Calls and puts options are popular in the financial markets.

Strike Price

The presence of a strike price is a common phenomenon in the trade of options. It can be described as a major component when it narrows down to penning down of an option contract. Options such as calls, and puts are heavily dependent on this factor. Its critical nature can be shown by an option trader who needs the call options. It is important because it determines the value possessed by the option. Several people have familiarized strike prices with a different name which is known as the exercise price.

Premium Price

The premium can be described as the price an option buyer in a contract pays the seller of the option. Terms of an option contract state that the amount is always paid upfront. It is always important for a trader to always remember that this component of a contract is not refundable. The rule extends itself to the side that one cannot be refunded his or her money even if the contract has been exercised. The premium quotation in a contract is always done in a certain way for efficiency. The most common way across the globe entails the quotation of option in the foundation of shares which is termed per share basis. The amount of premium is always affected by several variables before it is agreed on.

Expiration Date

One can easily understand the term expiration date of a contract as the last day he or she has the right to exercise either buying or selling the underlying financial instruments. A contract is termed worthless in moments the expiration date has passed. The expiration date tends to differ depending on the type of contract an individual has entered this despite the general principle of the contract being worthless after the last days.

Settlement Option

The settlement of options can be described as the process by which the holder and writer of an options contract resolve and exercise the terms stated. The process entails the participation of two parties in the trade of options and it differs depending on the options one has decided to trade.

Differences among Options, Forex, and Stocks

When it comes to forex trading, the entire system is totally different. Before you can trade using leverage, you need to have opened the forex trading account. That's the only requirement that is out there, nothing else. When you open a forex account, you can easily use the leverage feature. When you decide to trade stocks, you end up purchasing the companies' shares that have a cost from a few dollars down to even hundreds of dollars. Usually, the price in the market tends to share with demand and supply.

Paired trades

When you trade with forex, you are facing another world, unseen in the stock market. Though the currency of a country tends to change, there will always be a great supply of currency that you can trade. What this means is that the main currencies in the world tend to be very liquid.

When you are in forex trading, you will see that the currencies are normally quoted in pairs. They are not quoted alone. This means that you should be interested in the country's economic health that you have decided to trade in. The economic health of the country tends to affect the worth of the currency.

The basic considerations change from one forex market to another. If you decide to purchase the Intel shares, the main aim is to see if the stock's value will improve. You aren't interested in how the prices of other stocks are.

Price sensitivity to trade activities

When we look at both markets, we have no choice but to notice that there is varying price sensitivity when it comes to trade activities done.

If a small company that has fewer shares has about ten thousand shares bought from it, it could go a long way to impact the price of the stock. For a big company such as Apple, such n number of shares when bought from it won't affect the stock price. When you look at forex trades, you will realize that trades of a few hundreds of millions of dollars won't affect the major currency at all. If it affects, it would be minute.

Market accessibility

It is easy to access the currency market, unlike its counterpart, the stock market. Though you may be able to trade stocks every second of the day, five days weekly in the twenty-first century, it is not easy.

Chapter 1:

The Opportunity of Options Trading

Many novice traders have visions of making millions of dollars buying and selling individual call options. It is possible to make money trading individual call and put options, however very few professional traders make a career doing so. The fact is that straight trading of individual options is not likely to bring consistent and long-term success. It is just too difficult to consistently predict which way a stock price is going to move over short time periods.

That said, everyone has to start as a level 2 trader, and you can look at the period of time that you spend trading call and put options as a chance to gain some experience. At first, start with single options contracts until you get used to the mentality and experience of options trading.

As you train yourself, although many will be tempted to stick with call options because they are the way people think (you make money when the stock rises in price), you should also look for opportunities to make money from put options, and trade them. This will help your skills as an options trader broaden and improve, and you will start learning how to recognize trends in the markets that move in both directions.

Adopt a Trading Type

We haven't gotten into all the trading strategies yet. But by the time you finish this reading, you will understand all the main ways that you can trade options and the main strategies that are used by professional options traders. As you are learning, you can try your hand at all of them and find out which ones you enjoy the most and which ones you are best at trading.

However, you should winnow out your trading methods. The best professional traders are those that focus on using only one or two trading strategies. Options traders that become sellers of options premium typically only sell options premium. Of course, some people are able to multi-task more than others, and so they may have a more diversified strategy. The traders on Tasty Trade are often using many different strategies. That said, when you are a new options trader, it is good to find one or two strategies and then master them. If you can work up a solid profit over the course of a year, then at that time you might want to expand your trading repertoire.

As another example, many traders like using iron condors to generate income. A large number of traders only trade iron condors. They have become experts at using this one technique, and so they spend their time looking for opportunities to apply the strategy and earning regular income.

Equipment and Location

Most options traders don't need a large amount of equipment. If you start saying the word "trader," you are probably approaching this issue thinking of day traders with banks of computer screens displaying lots of charts and tables. This is not necessary for the vast majority of options traders. You certainly should have a good desktop computer that you have access to, and optionally you should also have a smartphone or tablet you have access to as well. If you are using a trading platform that does not have a lot of analysis tools and you have to use a second website for that purpose, you might want to have a second desktop computer or use a second device like an iPad to be following stock charts and so forth. Most traders can get by with a good desktop computer, iPad, and smartphone. And of course, you will need a good internet and Wi-Fi connection. The last thing you want to do is get in a situation where you are needing to get out of a trade and your internet connection goes down. This is one reason why having a smartphone so that you can still access the trading platform when your internet is down being a good idea, rather than relying exclusively on a desktop computer.

You can trade at home and then use a smartphone to keep tabs of your trading when not at home. It is recommended that you set aside a space for your trading activities. This is a part of viewing your options trading as a business. If you were to start an at-home business, you would probably set aside some home office space for it. Do the same when it comes to your options trading.

Trading as a Business

Options trading is flexible. You don't have to dive into options trading full time if you don't want to. You can do it very part-time, and set a goal of only making a few hundred dollars a month, or you can go full-fledged into options trading and try and build a million dollar a year business.

Trading as a business can, but doesn't necessarily have to, mean setting up an actual business for your trading activities. Depending on the laws of your location, you can setup a corporate entity and use that for your trading activities. Approaching it in that way will require satisfying all of the legal requirements, including tax forms, and setting up separate bank accounts.

Of course, it is not necessary to setup a business for options trading. You can certainly do it and just treat it as an individual income. Keep in mind that options trading – for the most part – is going to involve short term capital gains. In the United States short term capital gains are treated as regular income for tax purposes. If you do invest in LEAPs and hold some assets for a year or longer, you may be able to treat your gains as long-term capital gains and get preferential tax treatment.

You are unlikely to run into any legal trouble with the one exception being opening a margin account. If you open a margin account and are unable to meet your debt obligations, then you could get into some trouble. That might be something to consider when thinking about whether or not you start your trading activities as an official business to separate it from your personal activities. But for most people, it shouldn't be necessary to go through all the trouble of setting up a business when it comes to options trading.

Risk Management

One of the most important things to get a handle on when you begin trading options is a plan for risk management. On the losing side, this means having a "stop loss." That is a value you use to determine when to exit a trade. So, if the options price were to drop say $50, you can setup your trading platform to automatically sell any options that fit this description. Alternatively, you can also setup trades to automatically sell when you reach a certain level of profit. This is called "take profit." Check to see if your trading platform allows you to enter automatic stop loss and take profit orders.

If you can, this will greatly simplify your trading activities, and keep you from making impulsive and emotional mistakes. Instead, you will be able to cap your losses on any given trade, and ensure that if stock prices are rising, you get out with profits without waiting too long because you get excited and greedy. Remember, that can lead to losses. It is better to put caps, which of course means that you are going to miss out on some gains from time to time. But more often than not, it means that you are going to avoid making large mistakes. It is better to consistently make $50 profits, rather than holding on too long all the time hoping to score big and ending up with small profits or even losses.

If your system does not allow you to enter automatic stop loss and take profit orders, you are going to have to develop some personal discipline and manage those manually. That means that you would have to pay attention to your gains and losses, and be ready to exit trades when the rule you have decided upon is realized. There are no hard rules to follow, you will have to pick something that works for you. But in my opinion, on a per option basis, a maximum loss of $25 is reasonable. So, if you enter into a trade and you are losing $25 per options contract, you should go ahead and sell your options. This is a matter of cutting losses without letting them get out of control while you hope that things get better. Also, it will keep you from panicking too easily, by setting a fairly significant loss level, you will keep yourself from jumping out too early when the stock is going to reverse and make profits for your options.

On the other side, for take profit, take a 2-to-1 to 4-to-1 ratio. So, if you are going to have a $25 stop loss limit, then set your take profit to $50, or possibly $100, per options contract or trade. These rules are not going to guarantee profits. Sometimes they are going to work to provide winning trades, and sometimes this is not going to appear to help you. What you are looking for is a systematic approach that will help you to earn profits on average. The specific values you pick are less important than simply having some kind of risk management system. Of course, you don't want to be too conservative, because then you will be missing out on a lot of profits and getting out of many trades too early. And don't stop here. Remember that we said you should be aiming to continually educate yourself as an options trader. So, get online and find out what other options traders are doing, and settle on the type of risk management system that fits you the best. Remember that different traders are going to have different levels of risk tolerance.

Chapter 2:

Who Is This Book for?

This guide is perfect if you are interested or are actually beginning your journey into Options Trading.

When trading options for beginners, we deal with the basics, the foundation of a strong foundation in learning stock trading. With the right knowledge, you can make a huge profit with stock options. For beginners in options trading, it can be difficult to tell the exact difference between stock market trading and stock option trading.

Due to the deadlines set for each trade, many beginners of options trading have a common misconception that stock options carry high risks. The period is often perceived as a loss of assets. Options trading has proven to be advantageous because traders approach it with a plan and knowledge of effective leverage techniques. Options are usually selected for a level of leverage with limited risk.

Just as successful entrepreneurs must create a business plan, beginners in options trading should have a plan when joining a trading company. Exploring a topic is always a good idea; you can create a strategy around the knowledge gained by merely searching the internet! Coaching programs are also a great way to find free seminars or websites that allow guests free online courses.

Through these programs, called "Webinars," you can find free websites and many online forums to help beginners in options trading build a basic set of skills and find the opportunities you have available for further education, all within a monetary commitment.

As a beginner in options trading, your top priority when setting up a plan is to ask yourself what you hope to gain from trading options. Where is your risk tolerance? What does your portfolio look like? How big do you want to start with a collection? As a newbie, you can't expect the worst too soon. It's not about getting rich quick; trading takes time, patience, and a lot of perseverance if you hope to see a profit. You may have to go through various strategies and suffer some losses before you find a strategy that suits you, but you can minimize losses with the right set of skills.

When I started, I traded in stock options with virtually no knowledge, so I can help beginners avoid the same mistakes I made. In the beginning, I had very unrealistic expectations. I had experienced in the stock market, but when I switched to stock options, I had four reasons:

1.) Options can be bought and sold for a fraction of the base price of the shares.

2.) Without ownership of the underlying shares, you can still manage them using the share option.

3.) You can always use this option no matter how the stocks move.

4.) You can manage risks by securing a trading position.

I've had some grim experience, but perhaps I can help you understand why many beginners fail in the end. The biggest mistake I made when I first started was not properly researching coaching programs. I wanted to become an expert quickly, so I enrolled in a program that far exceeded my abilities. In the end, I had to learn again, because these were not options for beginners.

The basics are essential for a better understanding; I can't stress this enough; the key is to become a successful trader. Option trading always carries risk like any other investment, but based on the basics, you can minimize your risk and find success!

Options are treated as derivatives because these financial transactions are based on the value of assets or underlying securities. Unlike stocks, options expire on specific dates and do not have a fixed number specified for availability. Most people may not understand how options work, but some have used them in their business. Beginners should know that there are two types of options they can work on. The first of these is, for example, the possibility of calling them. You can buy stocks at a specific price before a certain date. This can be compared to buying deposits.

Merchants pay a premium for the purchase of calling options. This payment gives them the right to purchase the underlying asset in the future at a predetermined exercise price. For example, traders are not allowed to buy shares because they are not obliged but lost money in the form of an option premium during the process if they are waiting to expire. Another type of option they can trade is called a put option.

Traders can sell the underlying asset at an agreed price and on a specific day. Options, in this case, are comparable to insurance.

Traders can exercise their put options and sell assets at the insurance price. If the amount of the underlying asset increases, it does not have to exercise its put option, and the only cost incurred is the premium. Call and put settings are used by traders to reduce the risk of receiving them. Those who buy options have the right to exercise. Traders wishing to exercise their call option may purchase the underlying asset at a given exercise price, and those wishing to use their put option may sell it at an agreed price.

Although call and put sellers have the right to buy or sell, they are not obliged to do so. They may decide to exercise their rights, depending on their market analysis. There are several ways traders can set off their options, in addition to using their powers. They can dispose of it by buying or selling, or they can give it up. Traders may choose to give up their options if the remaining premium is lower than the cost of liquidation.

Chapter 3:

Why to Trade Options

There are several people who have found it appealing to trade in stocks because of its popularity. This is because several people fear trading other financial instruments. This is not supposed to be the case since other financial instruments such as options have a myriad advantage in the financial markets. Despite several people trading stocks, the numbers of people who are trading options have increased tremendously over the years. The major trigger of this increase is the advantages possessed by options. These advantages include;

Capital Outlay and Cost Efficiency

There is one of the major reasons that is owned by the trading of options. The talked about reason is the potential of making huge amounts of profits. It is more advantageous because an individual does not need to have huge capital investment in the trade. This phenomenon has made it ideal for an investor to focus on options trading because they can be able to start small as they invest more as time goes by. It is an attraction to even investors who have huge budgets as well because it proves to be cost-effective. In simple terms, one can be able to use leverage to acquire more trading power.

It is an occurrence that has been proved to be true in the financial market. It is in the sense that an option trader can be able to purchase options of similar stock. This will give him or her the power to purchase the stock by using a call option. Buying options and then buy shares, in the event he or she sells the shares in the present market situation, one can be in a position to make a huge amount of profits. The trade of options has certain positions an individual can take to make sure that he or she save his or her capita investment depending on the underlying asset.

Risk and Reward

The risk to reward advantage is often linked to the first advantage illustrated above. It is all narrows down to profits an individual is able to create in the options market. Traders and investors in the options markets can make proportionate gains with regards to the amount they have invested in the trade. A good depiction can be made from the potential an individual has to gunner from small investment which also has the potential of multiplying. The advantaged risk to reward ratio is achieved to its maximum potentials in the event that an individual uses the right strategies. It is important for an individual to constantly note that there will always be risks involved in options trading. This is because it is a characteristic of any form of investment or business done by any person. There are trading strategies that can be very risky when it comes to using them to base critical decisions such as those that are speculative. The general rule in options trading is that speculation with high potential returns tends to have high-risk involvement in it. On the other hand, options that have low-risk levels tend to have fewer amounts of gains. Options trading involves various types of options contracts. This makes it easy for an individual to limit risks in option trading depending on the contract he or she has settled on.

Flexibility and Versatility

Flexibility is one of the most appealing elements that options trading poses. It is often in contract to several forms that are resented as a passive investment while some are inactive forms. The common characterization here is that an individual is limited to making money or using other strategies. A good depiction can be used by an individual who buys stocks for the thought of building his or her portfolio so as to serve long term gains. Such an individual can be able to use two kinds of strategies. The first strategy will involve a trader focusing on the long term gains and purchasing a stock that has the potential to increase in value in the future. The second strategy will involve an options trader can choose to invest in stocks that give regular returns. Buy and hold is a strategy that has several techniques involved to help it to be a success.

However, the flexibility and versatility offered by the trading of options mean that an option trader has the potential of opening more opportunities. This means that a trader or investor of options has the ability to make profits in any kind of market condition. One is able to speculate price movements of foreign currencies, indices, and commodities. What this means is that a range of option trading strategies plays higher roles to a trader in the identification of other profitable ventures and being successful in them.

Chapter 4:

Options the Basics

For you to succeed, you need the basic knowledge of what you want to do for it will help you on how to do things the right way with less trouble. To fit in the options trading game, you need to know the basic knowledge about this type of trading to be on the safer side. We shall take a look at the strategies you can use, the types of options, how it works, and its drawbacks.

Strategies Used in Options Trading

Strategies are the set of guidelines you need to follow to achieve amazing results in what you are doing, and options trading has its strategies, too. Let us now dig deeper into a number of the strategies that you need to implement.

Covered call strategy. It is a market transaction where an individual, mostly an investor who is offering call options for sale, owns the same size as the market trade. It is executed when the individual with the long term asset writes the call options on the asset. Covered call strategy is a popular strategy because of its capability to minimize risks and promote income generation.

It is mostly applied when you, as an investor, have an asset with a short term and short position, wanting to hold it for long for you to receive the options premiums. A seller who has amazing knowledge on covered call strategy gets higher profits as compared to other strategies. The drawback of this strategy is that an individual does not receive full options premium when the stock rises above the strike price.

Long straddle strategy. This is an options strategy where a trader purchases an asset that has both the long standard options and put-call. Also, the agreed price plus the time of expiry are normally similar. This strategy generates massive profits by having long put and call options. The long call practice in the market happens when long put expires, and there is a rise in the price of the instrument. Moreover, the long put is practiced only in the fall of the stock's price scenario. You are advised to use this strategy when you think the volatility of the stock will be significant through the trade term. You suffer losses if your underlying stock comes in between the upper and lower breakeven point.

Short straddle strategy. It is a risky strategy that is the vice versa of the long straddle options strategy. As an investor, you are advised to apply this strategy when there are chances of low volatility in the market. You are likely to suffer from significant losses when the stock behaves significantly in the market. The investor generates income and holds on the premium when the stock behavior in the market does not have much change in either direction.

Long strangle strategy. How does long strangle strategy work? Here is the answer to it. An investor normally purchases out of money standard options and puts calls simultaneously on the instrument with a similar time of expiry. Out of the money call option is a call option with a lower market price than the price agreed on an asset. Conversely, out of the money put option is a market situation in the case that an asset has a price above the strike price.

Most of the investors who apply this strategy have the belief that the asset will have a huge change in its behavior but are not sure in which direction. It is a cheaper strategy with limited losses compared to straddle because of the options which are purchased out of the money.

Iron butterfly strategy. Iron butterfly strategy involves selling and purchasing an at the money put and also at the money call. All of the options normally have the same expiration dates on the asset. It is named after a creature because the short put and call are offered for sale at the middle strike price forming the body part of a butterfly, while the wings come into formation when the put and call options are purchased either above or below the middle strike price.

Most traders use this strategy when they believe there will be no changes in the stock's price within the time of expiry. You have a higher likelihood of getting huge profits when you are near the strike price in the middle.

Iron condor strategy. It is an options strategy that involves the sale of out of the money call and put spread on a similar instrument (preferably asset) with a similar date of expiration. It is created when the trader offers the out of the money put for sale and purchases another one of a lower strike price. Also, created by offering one out of the money call for sale and purchases another one of a higher strike price. The call and put spreads are normally of the same width. Many traders prefer this strategy because of the capability of generating huge credit on the same risk as compared to other options strategies.

Long call butterfly spread. In this type of strategy, a trader normally utilizes both bull and bear call spread strategies with three different strike prices on similar instruments and time of expiry. A trader normally purchases two contracts for options where one is of a greater agreed price than the other contract. Also, there is a sale of two other contract options at a price in the middle. The price agreed should be equivalent to the amount you get when you distinguish the top strike price and the lowest one.

Protective collar strategy. This strategy is exercised when you purchase a put and conversely write a call with the situation of out of the money in the market. It takes place on a similar stock with a similar time of expiry. Combining long put and the short call forms the collar of the stock, which is normally established by the agreed prices of the options. Its protective feature, moreover, comes up from the capability of the put option to offer protection on the stock until on the expiration of the option. Bear put spread trading strategy. A trader on this strategy buys put options at an agreed price then offers a similar amount of put for sale at a lower price. A similar type of option is on the same stock with the same date of expiration. Most bearish traders use this strategy with the expectations that the price of the stock will drop. The advantage of this strategy is its ability to offer minimal losses though it also offers minimal profits, which is a turn off for most traders.

Bull call strategy. You, as an investor, purchase calls at an agreed price and simultaneously offer the calls for sale at a greater agreed price. Normally happens in similar instruments having a similar time of expiration. Most bullish traders use this strategy expecting there will be an average increase in the price of the stock to gain profits.

Long put trading strategy. It is a bearish options trading strategy. An investor who uses this strategy expects the stock will move become lower before the time of expiration. Risks involved here are minimal to the amount of premium paid. The downside of this strategy is that the price of the asset must drop before the date of expiration, or else you lose all the option money. Short put trading strategy. Unlike the long put options strategy, a short put strategy is utilized mostly when the trader is bullish about the stock, that is, expects a rise in the stock's price. In any case, the agreed price becomes lower than that of the asset; then, the trader makes massive profits. The losses incurred here are unlimited.

Why Use Options?

Why should you use options? Here are a few reasons why you should utilize options as your tool for trading.

- You only need minimum initial cash outlay to purchase options as compared when buying stock in trading.

- Options such as call options enable investors to enter the market at a cheaper cost.

- Options also help investors to generate more income. It is seen mostly by using the covered call options trading strategy. The investor holds on to the stock believing the price will have few changes. As in, either to remain stable or increase a little.

• Purchasing calls and put options enable traders to invest with minimal risks since the major thing they can lose is premium.

• Using options will offer you more investment alternatives since it is a flexible trading tool.

How Options Work

After knowing the strategies and the reasons why to use options, let us now know how this type of trading works. Below are some of the details I have for you:

• Options have a time frame. They always have their date of expiration. You should be able to know their time frame to make profits. After they expire, you do not have the right to purchase or offer stock for sale at a specified price. The shorter the time it has till expiry, the lower the value of the option.

• Options have different strike prices, which normally indicate the price of the stock.

• Options offer you the right to purchase or offer stock for sale.

• Purchasing an option gives you the honor to purchase or offer the stock for sale.

• Selling an option gives you the honor of delivering the stock at an agreed price. The stock's current price is not under consideration.

Chapter 5:

What Is an Options Contract?

An options contract sounds fancy but it's a pretty simple concept.

- It's a contract. That means it's a legal agreement between a buyer and a seller.

- It gives the owner of the contract the opportunity to purchase or dispose of an asset with a fixed amount.

- The purchase is optional – so the buyer of the contract does not have to buy or sell the asset.

- The contract has an expiration date, so the purchaser – if they choose to exercise their right – must make the trade on or before the expiration date.

- The purchaser of the contract pays a non-refundable fee for the contract.

There are options contracts that take place in all aspects of daily life including real estate and speculation. A simple example illustrates the concept of an options contract.

Suppose you are itching to buy a BMW and you've decided the model you want must be silver. You drop by a local dealer and it turns out they don't have a silver model in stock. The dealer claims he can get you one by the end of the month. You say you'll take the car if the dealer can get it by the last day of the month and he'll sell it to you for $67,500. He agrees and requires you to put a $3,000 deposit on the car.

If the last day of the month arrives and the dealer hasn't produced the car, then you're freed from the contract and get your money back. In the event he does produce the car at any date before the end of the month, you have the option to buy it or not. If you really wanted the car you can buy it, but of course, you can't be forced to buy the car, and maybe you've changed your mind in the interim.

The right is there but not the obligation to purchase, in short, no pressure if you decided not to push through with the purchase of the car. If you decide to let the opportunity pass, however, since the dealer met his end of the bargain and produced the car, you lose the $3,000 deposit.

In this case, the dealer, who plays the role of the writer of the contract, has the obligation to follow through with the sale based upon the agreed-upon price.

Suppose that when the car arrives at the dealership, BMW announces it will no longer make silver cars. As a result, prices of new silver BMWs that were the last ones to roll off the assembly line, skyrocket. Other dealers are selling their silver BMWs for $100,000. However, since this dealer entered into an options contract with you, he must sell the car to you for the pre-agreed price of $67,500. You decide to get the car and drive away smiling, knowing that you saved $32,500 and that you could sell it at a profit if you wanted to.

The situation here is capturing the essence of options contracts, even if you've never thought of haggling with a car dealer in those terms.

An option is in a sense a kind of bet. In the example of the car, the bet is that the dealer can produce the exact car you want within the specified time period and at the agreed-upon price. The dealer is betting too. His bet is that the pre-agreed to price is a good one for him. Of course, if BMW stops making silver cars, then he's made the wrong bet.

It can work the other way too. Let's say that instead of BMW deciding not to make silver cars anymore when your car is being driven onto the lot, another car crashes into it. Now your silver BMW has a small dent on the rear bumper with some scratches. As a result, the car has immediately declined in value. But if you want the car, since you've agreed to the options contract, you must pay $67,500, even though with the dent it's only really worth $55,000. You can walk away and lose your $3,000 or pay what is now a premium price on a damaged car.

Another example that is commonly used to explain options contracts is the purchase of a home to be built by a developer under the agreement that certain conditions are met. The buyer will be required to put a non-refundable down payment or deposit on the home. Let's say that the developer agrees to build them the home for $300,000 provided that a new school is built within 5 miles of the development within one year. So, the contract expires within a year. At any time during the year, the buyer has the option to go forward with the construction of the home for $300,000 if the school is built. The developer has agreed to the price no matter what. So if the housing market in general and the construction of the school, in particular, drive up demand for housing in the area, and the developer is selling new homes that are now priced at $500,000, he has to sell this home for $300,000 because that was the price agreed to when the contract was signed. The home buyer got what they wanted, being within 5 miles of the new school with the home price fixed at $300,000. The developer was assured of the sale but missed out on the unknown, which was the skyrocketing price that occurred as a result of increased demand. On the other hand, if the school isn't built and the buyers don't exercise their option to buy the house before the contract expires at one year, the developer can pocket the $20,000 cash.

What Is an Options Contract on the Stock Market?

On the stock market, we are betting on the future price itself, and the shares of stock will be bought or sold at a profit if things work out. The key point is the buyer of the options contract is not hoping to acquire the shares and hold them for a long time period like a traditional investor. Instead, you're hoping to make a bet on the price of the stock, secure that price, and then be able to trade the shares on that price no matter what happens on the actual markets. We will illustrate this with an example.

1. Call Options

A call is a type of options contract that provides the option to purchase an asset at the agreed-upon amount at the designated time or deadline. The reason you would do this is if you felt that the price of a given stock would increase in price over the specified time period. Let's illustrate with an example.

Suppose that Acme Communications makes cutting edge smartphones. The rumors are that they will announce a new smartphone in the following three weeks that is going to take the market by storm, with customers lined out the door to make preorders.

The current price that Acme Communications is trading at is $44.25 a share. The current pricing of an asset is termed as the spot price. Put another way, the spot price is the actual amount that you would be paying for the shares as you would buy it from the stock market right now.

Nobody really knows if the stock price will go up when the announcement is made, or if the announcement will even be made. But you've done your research and are reasonably confident these events will take place. You also have to estimate how much the shares will go up and based on your research you think it's going to shoot up to $65 a share by the end of the month. You enter into an options contract for 100 shares at $1 per share. You pay this fee to the brokerage that is writing the options contract. In total, for 100 shares you pay $100.

The price that is paid for an options contract is $100. This price is called the premium. You don't get the premium back. It's a fee that you pay no matter what. If you make a profit, then it's all good. But if your bet is wrong, then you'll lose the premium. For the buyer of an options contract, the premium is their risk.

You'll want to set a price that you think is going to be lower than the level to which the price per share will rise. The price that you agree to is called the strike price. For this contract, you set your strike price at $50.

Remember, exercising your right to buy the shares is optional. You'll only buy the shares if the price goes high enough that you'll make a profit on the trade. If the shares never go above $50, say they reach $48, you are not obligated to buy them. And why would you? As part of the contract deal, you'd be required to buy them at $50.

We'll say that the contract is entered on the 1st of August, and the deadline is the third Friday in August. If the price goes higher than your strike price during that time, you can exercise your option.

Let's say that as the deadline approaches, things go basically as you planned. Acme Communications announces its new phone, and the stock starts climbing. The stock price on the actual market (the spot price) goes up to $60.

Now the seller is required to sell you the shares at $50 a share. You buy the shares, and then you can immediately dispose of these at a quality or optimal amount, or $60 a share. You make a profit of $10 a share, not taking into account any commissions or fees.

2. The Call Seller

The call seller who enters into the options contract with the buyer is obligated to sell the shares to the buyer of the options contract at the strike price. If the contract sets the strike price at $50 a share for 100 shares, the seller must sell the stock at that price even if the market price goes up to any higher price, such as $70 a share. The call seller keeps the premium. So, if the buyer doesn't exercise their option, the call seller still gets the money from the premium.

Chapter 6:

Call and Put Options

P ut and call options are referred to as a derivative investment. The movements of their prices depend on the movements of prices of a different financial product, also referred to as the underlying.

So, what is an option? It is defined as the right to sell or buy a certain stock with a set price given a specific time frame. With options, you won't have outright ownership of the shares, but you make calculated bets on a stock's price and what its value will be in the future, given the specified expiration of the option. What makes options attractive is that you are to choose whether you want to exercise them or not. If your bet is wrong, you can let the options expire. Although the options' original cost is lost, it still wouldn't compare had you paid for the stock's full price.

Call options are purchased when the trader is expecting the underlying's price to go up within a particular time frame.

Put options are purchased when the trader is expecting the underlying's price to go down within a particular time frame.

There's an option for puts and calls to be written or sold. This will still generate income, but certain rights have to be given up to the option's buyer.

For options defined for the US, a call is defined as an options contract giving the buyer rights to buy an underlying asset at a set price any time until the expiration date. For options defined for the EU, buyers can choose to exercise the option to purchase the underlying but only on the set expiration date.

The strike price is defined as a determined beforehand at which the call buyer has the choice to purchase the underlying asset. For example, a buyer of a certain stock call option with a 10$ strike price may opt to purchase that stock at the same price before the expiration date of the option.

The expiration of options may vary. It can also be short or long term. It can be worth the while for call buyers to exercise the option, which is to require the writer or seller of the call to sell the stocks at the set strike price., but only if the underlying's current price is more than the strike price. For example, if a stock trades at $10 at the stock market, it is not profitable for the buyer of the call option to exercise the choice to purchase that stock at $11 since they could get the same on the market at a lower price.

Put buyers reserve the right to sell stocks at strike price during a set time range.

The highs and lows the stock market goes through can be both exciting and nerve-wracking for newbie or veteran investors. Risking hard-earned money can make anyone anxious. But played right with sound and well-planned strategies, you can be successful in this field

If you are looking for a way to invest in the stock market but you are trying to avoid the risk of directly selling stocks or buying them, options trading might be perfect for you. Options are typically traded at significantly lower prices compared to the underlying prices of the actual shares. This makes trading them a less risky way to control a large stock position, although you don't own the shares. Using options strategically allows risk mitigation while maintaining huge profit potentials, and you will be playing in the field even if you're investing just a fraction of the stock's price.

All of these benefits of options trading got you excited, right? After all, options have a lower risk and they're a lot cheaper. There are two major disadvantages, however – the limited-time aspect and the reality that you don't own the stock until you choose to exercise your options.

Call Options

With call options, what you pay for is just 'rights to buy' certain shares at a set price and covered by a specific time frame. Let's say that stock ABC is selling for $90 per share in May. If you believe that the stock's price will go up over a few months, you'd purchase a three-month option to buy 100 shares of ABC by August 31 for $100. For this sample call option, you would be paying around $200 if the option cost per share is $2. In options, you are only allowed to buy in increments of 100 shares. This gives you the choice to purchase 100 shares of ABC anytime within the three-month timeframe. The $200 investment is significantly lower than the $9,000 you would have had to shell out if you bought 1000 shares outright.

If you bet right and on July 15, if the ABC shares hit the market at $115, you may exercise the call option and you would have gained $1,300 (that's 100 shares multiplied by the $15 profit you gained per share and deducted by your original investment of $200). If you don't have the resources to buy the shares, you can also make a profit if you re-sell the option to another investor or via the open market. The gain will be pretty much similar to this option.

If you bet wrong, and the price of ABC's shares fell to $80 never to reach $100 within the three-month timeframe, you can let the option reach its expiration, which saves you money (if you bought the shares outright, your original investment of $9,000 is now down to a value of only $8,000, so you lost $1000). This means you only lost $200, which was your investment for the call option.

Risks Involved in Call Options

Like any other form of investment, options have their share of potential risks. Taking the second scenario where you bet wrong as an example and stock ABC never got to $100 during the option's timeframe of three months, you would have lost the entire $200 of your investment, right? In terms of loss percentage, that's %100. Anyone who's been playing the stock market would tell you that it's extremely rare for an investor to suffer a 100% loss. This scenario can only happen if ABC suddenly went bankrupt, causing the price of their stocks to plummet down to zero value.

Therefore, if you look at it from a point of view of percentages, options can cause you huge losses. Let's elaborate on this point. If the price of

ABC's share went up to $99 and it's the last day for you to exercise the option, choosing to purchase the shares will mean losing a dollar for each share. What if you invested $9,000 for the stock and you owned 100 stock shares? In three months, which is the option's expiration date if you took it, you would have gained 10% from your original investment ($99 from $90). Comparing both, you would have gained 10% if you purchased the shares outright and lost %100 if you chose the option but did not exercise it. This example shows how risky options can be.

However, the opposite can happen if stock ABC reached a price higher than $100. If you purchased the option, your gain percentage would have been substantially higher compared to buying the stocks outright. If the stock reached $110, you would have gained 400% ($10 gain versus the $2 per share investment) if you went for the option and only gained 22% ($20 gain versus the $90 per share investment) if you purchased the shares.

Lastly, when you own the stock, nothing can force you to sell. That means if after three months, and stock ABC's price goes down, you can hang on to it if you believe it still has the potential to recover and even increase in value compared to the original. If the price goes up dramatically, you'll make significant gains and you didn't incur losses. However, if you chose options as your investment method, the expiration would have forced you to suffer a 100% loss after the set timeframe. There will be no option to hold on to the stock even if you believe it will go up in value soon.

Options have major pros and also major cons. You need to be aware of these before you step into the arena of options trading.

Put Options

On the other side of the options investment is the put option. Whereas call is the right to purchase, 'put' gives you the option to sell a certain security at a set price within a specific time frame. Investors usually purchase put options to protect the price of a stock in case it suddenly drops down, or even the market itself. With put options, you can sell the shares and your investment portfolio is protected from unexpected market swings. Put options are, therefore, a way to hedge your portfolio or lower its risk.

For example, you have invested in stock ABC for 100 shares, which you bought for $50 per share. As of May 31, the price per share has reached a market high $70. Of course, you'd want to maintain this position in your stock, and at the same time protect your gained profits in case the price of this stock goes down. To fit your requirements, you may purchase a put option with a three-month expiration and $70 per share strike price.

If ABC's stock price goes down drastically over the coming couple of months, reaching a low per-share price of only $60, you will still be protected. By exercising your put option, you will still be able to sell the shares at $70 each even if stock ABC is now trading at a lower value. If you are feeling confident that ABC can still recover in the future, you can hold on to the stock and just resell the put option. The price of this put option will have gone up because of the diving stock ABC took.

On the other hand, if stock ABC's value kept climbing, just let the put option expire and you would still profit from the increased price of the shares. Even though you lost what you have invested in the put option, you still have the underlying stock with you. Therefore, you can view the put option as a kind of insurance policy for your investment, which may or may not use. Another thing to remember is that you can purchase put options even if you don't own the underlying stock, just like you would in a call option. You are not required to own the stock itself.

Risks Involved in Put Options

Just as with call options, put options carry the same risks. There is also a 100% loss potential when the underlying stock price goes up, and a huge gain when the price dives because you can resell the option for a higher price.

Chapter 7:

Derivative Contracts

O ptions are a group of conditional derivative contracts, which means that they are derivative financial instruments. The main role of derivatives in the financial market is the transfer of risk. Therefore, there is a commodity or a financial instrument, or any assets that have marketability, and from whose price depends on the price of derivatives that are traded on the derivatives market or futures market. Many derivatives are used to reduce risk. For example, a farmer who is not sure what will be the price of corn at harvest and sales. To remove this uncertainty, it is protected by derivatives of corn futures prices fall, thus avoiding the high losses. The basic role of the derivatives is the transfer of risk to participants who are willing to accept that risk and achieve huge profits/losses, as their forecasts of future price movements opposing those who want to protect themselves from risk. Participants who want to protect themselves from the risk are called hedgers, and those who accept that risk, and by realized profits/losses, are called traders (traders) which are popularly called speculators. Exchange-traded options include the right to buy or sell an asset, and the ability to withdraw from this right are the basic elements that make a difference between the options and futures.

The futures market or the market of derivatives would not be able to function, without a large number of speculators who are always willing to "gamble." Some financial institutions tend to use derivatives as a source of income. This is a general reason of famous incident involving the collapse of Barings Bank in February 1995. But not just Barrings Bank dealt with difficulties. Great financial difficulties also had Procter & Gamble, Orange Country, Hammersmith, and Fulham Local Authority. In the case of Barings Bank, Nick Leeson was obviously trying to take advantage of small differences in the prices of financial instruments which he bought on the stock markets of the Far East and sell them in other markets, trying to use a process known as arbitrage. In January and February 1995, he bet on Japanese stocks by buying a significant amount of futures contracts on the Nikkei 225 index on the stock exchanges in Osaka and Tokyo. There was a difficult period on the Japanese stock market which resulted in the disaster of the Barings Bank.

Options are the right to buy or sell a particular subject, such as stocks or government bonds at a predetermined price within a specified time limit.

the right to buy or sell an asset, and the ability to withdraw from this right are the basic elements that make a difference between the options and futures. Futures involve the need to sell an asset, on a certain day, at a specified price, if it did not "come out" of the contract. An option is considered to be a contract between the seller and the buyer in which he holds the right to buy or sell a financial instrument at a certain period of time or on a specified date in the future at a price specified at the moment of conclusion of the contract. The subject of the contract contained an option is called the basic investment (underlying asset). The subject of the contract can be:

• Goods (commodities) — agricultural products such as wheat, oil, wood, various metals, etc.

• Currency (currency)

• Action (stock, equities)

• Futures contracts (futures contracts)

• Stock indices (indexes) the price of the contract which is determined at the time of conclusion of the contract or the price at which the assets, which is the subject of an optional contract, may be bought or sold, is called the exercise price (strike price, exercise price). The strike price or exercise price of those options is usually very close to the current price of assets and it is subject to an optional contract, except in cases of exceptional growth or falling prices.

It is because the stock market is determining the strike price based on various analyses of the current market. Options are available in several amounts above or below the current price (current price, spot price) of the underlying investments. For example, stock prices that are below $ 25 per share usually have strike prices in the range 2½. The strike price of shares above $ 50 is generally in the range of $ 5. As for the share option, they are not available in every action. There are about 2,200 shares on which options are traded. Options are traded on stock exchanges around the world: LIFFE (London International Financial Futures and Options Exchange) -London, CBOE-Chicago, EUA-

European stock market option, MONEY-France, and Deutsche Boerse and Eurex (German-Swiss international derivatives market) have opened a segment dedicated to the American actions. The opening of new markets in the segment of the Deutsche Boerse is intended to the best American actions-Xetra US Stars. Here we can find all the US stocks from the Dow 3ones Industrial Average, the S & P 100, Dow and NasdaqlOO 3ones Global Titans 50. On the same day, Eurex introduced options trading on stocks on denominated in the euro at 10 US stocks. These US stocks on which options can be found are AOL Time Warner, Cisco Systems, Citigroup, EMC, General Electric, IBM, Intel, Microsoft, Oracle and Sun Microsystems. The introduction of options on the most liquid US stocks, helped the Eurex to develop an even greater extent in its segment of options trading. Derivatives based on stocks are offering a significant increase in value and have great potential for growth. Investors are expecting from the leading stock markets to offer intelligent products for derivatives based on stocks, as well as for the American risk management instruments. London International Stock Exchange of futures and options-LIFFE announced that the total turnover of non-financial products traded in October 2001, was 16% higher than the same period last year. They traded with 395,103 contracts, compared to 341,249 in October 2000. The traffic increased in September when it was traded 369,464 contracts. The largest percentage of growth was recorded at the trade agreements with the ground in barley and coffee. Vendor of the options, or actually the side of the contract which must implement its obligation, in the case that the buyer (purchaser/ holder) of the option wishes that the contract to be implemented, is called the issuer. The date in the contract that represents a term in which the option matures and after which no longer applies is called the expiration date, and it is usually the third Friday of the month when the option expires. Expiration dates can vary from one month to three years in the case of LEAPS (Long-term Equity Anticipation Securities) options. If a customer wants to use the rights that the option provides, he has to pay an appropriate price, which is called the premium (premium). The premium is the price of an option and it is determined by many factors such as type of the basic investment, the current price, the rate of price volatility of the underlying investments in the prior year, current interest rate, the strike price of the option, and the time remaining until the expiration of the option. In a case of share options, the premium is calculated by the per-share method. Each option correspondent with the number 100. So, in case the premium is $2, the total premium for an option would be $200 ($ 2 x 100= 200$).

Chapter 8:

The Options Are a Flexible Tool

I f you were to first open your contract by selling, we say that you are "short." If you buy to open a position, we say that you are "long." The simplest way to trade options is to take a long position on a call or a put. Although when buying and selling stocks we say that someone "shorts" the stock when they are hoping to profit off a decline in share price, you can be hoping to profit from a decline in share price, but you are "long" with regard to the put option.

The strategy for profiting from going long on a call or put option is simple. You are hoping the price of the stock would move in your favor so that you will earn a profit. The industry is full of naysayers that downplay this basic strategy, however, the reality is you can definitely earn profits in this way. That is buying or selling individual options, be they the call or put variety. The key to success when doing this type of trading is to stay on top of it and don't buy options on a whim. You need a good reason to buy a call or a put option by itself, and that means paying attention to the financial news surrounding the company, earnings reports, and looking at simple market trends to determine when you have a reasonable probability of earning a profit.

Reading the Charts

As an options trader, you are going to have to learn how to read charts. The first thing to do is look up candlestick patterns so that you can recognize when a trend reversal might be coming. Candlestick patterns are not absolute rules or truth-tellers; they are an indicator. So you take the candlestick charts into consideration and use the entirety of the information that you have available to make your decisions.

As we said earlier, a candlestick can be divided into different timeframes. If you are looking to ride a trend over a single day, a five-minute timeframe is good to use. In this case, each candlestick is going to tell you what the price action was over the five-minutes period.

The candlesticks are going to be colored green or red. If a candlestick is green, it's a "bullish" candlestick. That means that over the period of interest, the closing price had risen to a larger higher than the opening price. By itself, it does not tell you where the price is headed. For a bullish candlestick, the top of the candle is the price at the end of the trading session, and the bottom of the body is the price at the start.

Each candlestick has "wicks" that come out of the top and bottom of the candlestick. The top wick gives you the high price for the time interval. The bottom candlestick gives you the low price of the time interval.

If a candlestick is red, that is a "bearish" candlestick. In that case, this means that the closing price was lower than the opening price. So, the top of the body is the opening price in this case, and the bottom of the body is the closing price (the price closed lower than it opened at). The meaning of wicks is the same.

A complete investigation of candlesticks is beyond the scope of this reading, so please see online resources or readings specifically addressing the topic, or day trading, to learn the patterns that you need to be looking for.

That said, here are the general rules for entering and exiting trades.

In the event of big news that you know is going to cause a massive move in the share price, you want to just get in early in the trading day.

If you are looking at a stock under normal conditions, that is no earnings report or other huge news, you want to wait for a downtrend in the share price so that you can enter a position at a relative minimum. So you buy the option at the lowest possible price given current market conditions. Then you wait until the price rises and the trend peaks out, and you close your position.

For beginners, I have to say get ready for the ride. If you are thin-skinned, this kind of trading is going to put you on pins and needles. As you know, stock prices do not follow a steady curve, they move up and down a lot. And as we have mentioned several times, a small move in share price which really isn't all that significant can have a big impact on options prices. It's not uncommon to get into a trade and see your option lose $75 or $100 over the course of a couple of hours, and then see it rise to a $50 or $100 profit in a few hours. So, this is not something for the faint of heart to get involved with.

But to avoid panic, you should rely on the indicators to help you make your decisions rather than relying on emotion.

The second big tool you need to use in your trading is the moving average. I like to use a 9-period case. This will be for an exponential moving average. Then for the long one, I will use twenty periods. Again, it will be an exponential moving average on the same chart. Moving averages average out the stock prices to give you smooth curves that show the overall price trend. Using two moving averages allows you to get signals when a trend is going to reverse. This actually works quite well in practice. The signal for a reversal is when the moving averages cross.

If a short period moving average crosses above a long period moving average, this is taken to be a signal of a coming uptrend. So in my case, I look for the 9-period moving average to cross above the 20-period moving average. This can be used to either reinforce your conviction that you should say in the trade or to enter a trade if you are looking to take advantage of a coming price movement (for call options).

If the short period moving average crosses below the long period moving average, that means that a downward trend is coming. So, if you have been riding a trend with a call option, that might be an indicator to sell to close your position.

You can also add a tool called the RSI to your charts, which is the relative strength indicator. This tells you if a stock is overbought or oversold. If the RSI is 70 or above, then the stock is considered to be overbought, and that can be a good time to exit a long call position. If the RSI is 30 or below, this is "oversold," and so it can be a good time to enter a long position for call options. I take the RSI with a grain of salt because I've seen it indicate overbought conditions which were then followed by continually rising prices, all too often. But it's one thing that you can consider looking at.

Finally, there are the Bollinger bands. These give you a moving average along with the standard deviation both above and below the moving average. If you are going to use this, the main reason would be to establish levels of support and resistance. A level of support is a low price level that the stock is unlikely to break below over a short time period. A level of resistance is the maximum price you are likely to see for the stock over a short time period. These are guidelines, a stock might suddenly break out of a range at any time.

Another reason to use Bollinger bands is for a guideline when selling to open a position. In this case, you could use one or two standard deviations to give you a boundary above and below which it's extremely unlikely the stock price is going to move. We will talk more about that in a few.

Having a Trading Plan

Having a trading plan in place is going to be important no matter what you do in the stock market. A trading plan should include the following:

- Your overall goal. This can include your reasons for investing as well as your goal for annual profits or ROI (return on investment).

- How much you are willing to put at risk. It should go without saying that you shouldn't bet the family farm on your trades. Set aside a fixed amount of money that you are willing to lose. If you are smart about your trading, you are unlikely to lose all of it, and hopefully, you don't have a string of losing trades. With options, you can start small and learn the ropes without risking large amounts of money. So start with something like $500. If you lose $500, it's not going to be the end of the world. If that happens, you can replenish it, and it's probably not going to put you in a position where you can't eat.

- Have a take profit level for the trade. This is done on a per-contract basis. The level I like to use is $50. It's true that you are going to miss out on some big gains some of the time, but having a fixed level ensures that overall you have a string of profitable trades. Remember that it is per contract, so you can trade five contracts on the same option and if you reach the $50 profit level, that is $250 in overall profit.

- Have an exit strategy. This is a personal tolerance level of risk. For me, it's a $100 loss on one contract, provided there are no signs of a turnaround coming. This is harder to quantify because options move up and down by large amounts over short time periods. So, if you are not somewhat flexible, getting out on a price move that is too small is going to cause you to lose out on a lot of trades. Remember that a $100 loss on a trade is only a price movement of

$1-$2 on the underlying stock. It goes without saying that a stock that drops by $1 is just as likely to reverse course and go up by $1.

- Always watch time decay. You can profit on options at any time, but if you buy an option that you intend to hold for a period of several days, potential losses from time decay must be taken into account. One mistake that beginners make is not paying attention to time decay.

- Never let options expire. Another beginner's mistake is to buy options and just hold onto them waiting to see what's going to happen. Never hold onto an out of the money option. Even if you are going to sell it for a large loss, get out of it if the expiration date is approaching. When it comes to in the money options, you might sell the day before expiration. You are probably not going to want to keep an in the money option past that unless you want it exercised.

Chapter 9:

Make Profit from the Call

The goal when purchasing options contracts is to buy a stock at a price that is lower than its current market value. In other words, you want the stock price to be significantly higher than the strike price so that you're enjoying significant savings in purchasing the stock. When evaluating your options, you'll need to take into account the added costs of the premium paid plus commissions. In some cases, commissions can be substantial so make sure you know what they are ahead of time so that you choose a good strike price and exercise your options at the right time.

You're a trader, not an investor

You may be mentally conditioned to think in terms of investing. An investor wants to build a diversified portfolio over a long time period that they believe will increase in value over the long term. A trader operates in the same universe but has different goals. You are after short term profits – not investments. You are not going to hold this stock. If you were interested in holding the stock, you would simply buy it at the lower price that is currently on offer. Your goal is to be able to buy at the strike price when the stock has increased significantly in price and then sell it immediately so that you can pocket the profits.

Let's take an example. Suppose that XYZ corporation is currently selling at $30 a share. People are expecting the stock to rise, and some people are really bullish about their short-term prospects. If you are an investor, your goal is to get the stock at the lowest possible price and then hold it long term. If you are using strategies like dollar-cost averaging, you might be buying a few shares every month without paying too much attention to what the price is specifically on the day you purchase. In any case, as an investor, you'll simply buy the shares at $30.

As a trader, you're hoping to cash in on the moves of XYZ over the coming couple of months. You'll buy an options contract, let's say its premium is $0.90 and the strike price is $35. Your cost for the 100 shares is $90.

Then the stock price shoots up to $45. Since it passed the strike price, you can exercise your option to buy the shares at the strike price. You can buy them at $35 for a total price of $3,500. But remember — you're not an investor in for the long haul. You'll immediately unload the shares. You sell the shares for $4,500 and make a $1,000 profit. After considering your premium, your profit is $910. It will go a little bit lower after considering commissions, but you get the idea. The purpose of buying call options is to make fast profits on stocks you think are going to spike.

It's hard to guess when the best time is to really buy call options. Obviously, you don't want to do it when a major recession hit. The optimal time is during a bull market, or when a specific company is expected to hit on something big, that will suddenly increase its value in the markets. A good time to look is also when a recession hits, but it passes the bottom out period.

Benefits of Buying Call Options

Call options have many benefits that we've already touched on earlier. In Particular:

- Call options allow you to control 100 shares of stock without actually investing in the 100 shares — unless they reach a price where you get the profit that you want.

- Call options allow you to sit and wait, patiently watching the market before making your move.

- If your bet doesn't work out, you're only going to lose a small amount of money on the contract. In our example, if XYZ loses value, and ends up at $28 per share instead of moving past your strike price of $35, then you're only out the $90 you paid for the premium.

- Call buying provides a way to leverage expensive stock.

What to Look for When Buying Call Options

Now let's take a look at some factors that you'll be on the lookout for when buying call options. You're going to want to be able to purchase shares of the stock you're interested in at a price that is less than the price you think it will go up to. You need to do this in order to ensure that the stock price surpasses the strike price. Of course, it's impossible to know what the future holds so this will involve a bit of speculation.

You'll have to do a lot of reading and research to make educated guesses on where you expect the stock to go in the coming weeks or months.

Second, you'll need to take into account the cost of the premium when making your estimates. For the sake of simplicity, suppose that you find a call option with a premium of $1 per share. You're going to need a strike price that is high enough to take that into account. If you go for a stock that is $40 a share with a $1 premium and a strike price of $41, obviously you're not going to make anything unless the stock price goes higher than $41. Remember that exercising your rights on the options contract is not a path toward immediate money. You're going to have to turn around and sell it ASAP in order to profit. Of course, when you sell is a judgment call as is when you exercise your right to buy. You're going to want to wait until the right moment to buy, but it's impossible to really know what that right moment is. This is where trading experience helps and even then, the most skilled experts can make mistakes. For a beginner, the best thing to do is exercise your right to buy the shares and then sell them as soon as they've gone far enough past the strike price for you to make a profit and cover the premium. If you wait too long, there is always the chance that the stock price will start declining again, and it will go below your strike price and never exceed it again before the contract expires.

Open Interest

If you get online to check stocks you're interested in, one of the measures you will see is "Open Interest." This tells you the number of open or outstanding derivative contracts there are for that particular stock. Every time that a buyer and seller enter into an options contract, this value increases by one. What you want to do with open interest as a trader looking to make real cash from call options is to look for stocks that show big movement in the number of open trades. You're going to want to look for increasing numbers. This means that other traders have an interest in buying call options on this stock and that they're expecting it to go up in value in the near future.

Of course, you're going to want to take an educated approach to this. Simply getting online and going through random stocks will be a waste of time, it might take you weeks to find something.

You're going to want to prepare ahead of time by keeping an eye on the financial news. Watch Fox Business, read the Wall Street Journal, and watch CNBC and read any other financial publications that are to your liking. Find out what stocks the experts are talking about and which ones they expect to make significant moves over the coming weeks and months. Keep in mind these people and experts often make mistakes, so you're only using it as a guideline. You also don't want to focus solely on looking for stocks that are going to make moves; you want to keep up with company news. You need to keep your ears open for news such as the development of a new drug or the latest electronic gadget. Sometimes you might find out news about that before the stock begins attracting a lot of interest in the markets.

Tips for Buying Call Options

- Don't buy a call option with a strike price that you don't think the stock can beat.

- Always include the premium price in your analysis.

- Look for calls that are just in the money. These are likely to bring a modest profit.

- Call options that are out of the money might give you an option for a cheaper premium.

- However, the premium shouldn't be your primary consideration when looking to buy a call option. Compared to the money required to buy the shares and the potential profits if the stock goes past the strike price, the premium is going to be a trivial cost in most cases – provided of course the strike price is high enough to take the premium into account.

- Look at the time value. If you're looking for larger profits, it's better to aim for longer contracts. Remember, that with any call option you have the option to buy the stock at the strike price at any time between today's date and the deadline when the stock market price exceeds the strike price. Longer time frames mean you increase the chances of that happening. Even if the price goes a little above the strike price and dips down, with a longer window of time before the deadline, you can wait and see if it rebounds. Remember if it never does, you're only out the premium.

- Start small. Beginning traders shouldn't bet the farm on options. You'll end up broke if you do that. The better approach is to start by investing in one contract at a time and gaining experience as you go.

Chapter 10:

Strike Price

The strike price is one of the most important if not the most important thing to understand when it comes to option contracts. The strike price will determine whether the underlying stock is actually bought or sold at or before the expiration date. When evaluating any options contract, the strike price is the first thing that you should look at. It's worth investigating the concept and how it's utilized in the actual marketplace.

The strike price will let you home in on the profits that can be made on an options contract. It's the break-even point but also gives you an idea as to your profits and losses. Of course, the seller always gets the premium no matter what.

For a call contract, the strike price is the price that must be exceeded by the current market price of the underlying equity. For example, if the strike price is $100 on a call contract, and the current market price goes to any price above $100, then the purchaser of the call can exercise their right at any time to buy the stock. Then the stock can be disposed of with a profit. Suppose that the current price rises to $130. Then you can exercise your option to buy the stock at $100 a share, and then turn around and sell it on the market for $130 a share, making a $30 profit per share before taking into account the premium and other fees that might accrue with your trades. While as the buyer of the contract you have no obligations other than paying the premium, the seller is obligated no matter what, and they must sell you the shares at $100 per share no matter how much it pains them to see the $130 per share price. Of course, there are reasons behind the curtain that will explain why they would bother entering this kind of arrangement that we will explore when an opportunity arises.

For a put contract, the strike price likewise plays a central role, but the value of the stock relative to the strike price works in the opposite fashion. A put is a bet that the underlying equity will decrease in value by a certain amount. Hence if the stock price drops below the strike price, then the buyer can exercise their right to sell the shares at the strike price even though the market price is lower. So, if your price is $100, if the current price of the equity drops to $80, the seller obligated to buy the 100 shares per contract from you at $100 a share even though the market price is $80 per share. In this case, you've made a gross profit of $20 a share.

The value of the strike price will not only tell you profitability but give you an indication of how much the stock must move before you are able to exercise your rights. Often when the amount is smaller, you might be better off.

When you know the strike price of different options contracts, then you can evaluate which one is better for you to buy. Suppose that a stock is currently trading at $80 and you find two options put contracts. One has a strike price of $75 and the other has a strike price of $60. Further, let's suppose that both contracts expire at the same time. In the first case, the stock price in the market will need to drop just $5 before the contract becomes profitable. For the second contract, it will have to drop $20.

The potential worth of each contract per share is the difference. For the contract with the $75 strike price, that is only $5. For the second contract with the strike price of $60, the potential worth is $20, four times as much.

Determining which contract is better is a matter of analysis and taking some risk. You can't just go by face value, but you must take into consideration the expiration date together with an analysis of what the stock will actually do over that time period. It may be that it's going to be impossible for the stock to drop $20 in order to make the second contract valuable. If the expiration date comes before the stock drops that much in price, the contract will be worthless. In other words, you'd never be able to exercise your option of selling shares at strike amount. On the other hand, even though there is not much discrepancy between the strike and the market amount for the first contract, and the market price might only drop to say $70 per share, the chances of this happening before the expiration date is more likely.

Your analysis might be different if the contract with the lower strike price has a longer expiration date.

The lesson to take to heart is that a stock is more likely to move by smaller amounts over short time periods. But the higher the risk, the more the potential profits.

Chapter 11:

How to Close an Options Contract

The entry point in a trade is the point at which you want to buy an asset. It's the starting bid in your trade. Whether you are trading stocks or options, you will always have to have an entry point. Having a good plan for when you will enter into a trade is really beneficial because it means that you won't have to drive yourself mad. It also means that you won't be making an emotional choice regarding when to enter.

Choosing a good entry point means analyzing the chart for support, resistance, and trend. Look at the past movement of the chart and find the support and resistance. Then, look at the trend. Has the chart been moving in a specific trend line? Or has it been in a stage of consolidation? Or a period where the market has remained fairly steady? With a stock that has a trend line, you can choose a point right after a rebound. For example, let's say stock ABC was trading at $60 in November before dropping to $58. As the number starts to rise again, you can see if the chart seems like it's going to return to trend. If yes, then you can place your entry point at $60 and wait to see if the trend will continue upward.

In the case of a stock that is at a stage of neutral movement, then your support and resistance lines will be horizontal, and the chart will remain between those two lines. In this case, follow the pattern of the prior movement and again place your entry point at the price where a rebound is likely to happen. This should be close to the support line. There's a good chance that the stock value will rise again towards the resistance in this case.

Let's put this into action. Chose two different practice charts. One should have a stock that is trending upwards, and one should have stock that is steady and isn't trending in a particular direction. Taking the one that is trending upward, draw the trend line in the support line position. From there, choose a position that offers you a small swing up. At what point would you enter the swing? At what price point? How long would you remain in the swing? Do the same for the chart that is remaining steady. What point above the support line would you enter into the trade? It's easy to do this with past charts because everything is already lined up. But take the time to analyze the chart. What makes specific swings more successful and what makes them unsuccessful?

Now try with a practice future trade. Again, find a chart from a stock that you would be interested in purchasing. Map out your lines, find the zone you'll trade in, and then choose an entry point either in the present or the future. After that, watch the stock for the upcoming several days. Would your trade have panned out? If yes, why? And if no, why not? All of this practice gives you the opportunity to try out trades before investing any capital into it. Once you feel a bit more confident about entry points, move on to learn about exit points.

When you enter into the trade, you need to make sure that your risk/reward ratio makes the trade worth it. Once you calculate the ratio, you can determine at what point you can exit the trade in order to make the reward worth it.

Now we're going to learn how to exit a trade. It is very important to have an exit strategy. Without an exit strategy, you will choose to leave a trade whenever you feel like it, which can cause you some losses. You may exit too early or too late. It is better to have a strategy in place so that you know exactly when you'll exit. For example, if you determine that you would like to make a specific amount of profit, that's your exit point. Don't go past that.

As you throw it, momentum keeps it going higher but at a slower pace until it reaches its peak. At this point, momentum is zero and the ball falls back to your hands. In a swing trade, you want to exit the trade before the momentum reaches zero. Not at the peak, but before the peak. This is because most traders will be looking to sell at the peak of the trade, which will cause a drop in the market. Selling early before the estimated peak is a risk. It might mean that you lose out if the ball continues to go much higher than you anticipated. However, you will still have made a gain before any reversal happens and you can always buy back into the trend if you want to.

When looking at the charts for a stock, you should keep in mind your entry position and where you would like to exit. If the stock has stayed steady over the last bit of time and remains in its range, then looking at the support and resistance can give you a good idea of where to exit. If you entered near the support, then you can determine at what point you would like to exit. This depends on a lot of factors like your tolerance for risk and how long you want to stay in the trade. Generally speaking, if the stock value keeps increasing, you want to exit before it hits the resistance. Remember, in swing trading, it's all about small gains, not large ones so it's better to leave with some profit rather than no profit.

With your support and resistance marked on a chart, you can also look for key indicators that show you that it's time to sell. One of these indicators is either if the stock value exceeds its resistance, or if it drops below its support numbers. This can mean that it's starting to trend in one specific direction, but it could also mean that these little breakouts will backtrack into the range it was sitting at before. If the stock value exceeds its resistance and you haven't sold yet, then you can choose to wait until it returns to its range or see if it will be the start of a new trend. This decision, again, depends on how much risk you're willing to take.

There are a couple of things you can do to make sure that you are not staying in a trade too long. The first one is to set a stop-loss. A stop-loss is a tool that will sell your shares in the event that the stock price goes too low. The other option is to set a limit order. A limit order will sell your trades once they've reached your set peak value. Let's say that the current stock price for ABC is $20 per share when you enter. You can choose to set your limit order at $25 a share. You can also set it at a certain percentage point for profit. This means that at the $25 mark, your broker will sell your shares. This can be good because it can limit your losses, but it can also prevent you from taking advantage of a possible trend. So once again, make a decision based on your tolerance for risk.

As you make your exit strategy, you should ask yourself a few questions. You should know how long you are willing to stay in a trade, how much risk you can tolerate and at what point you want to get out. These three things will help you make a good exit strategy. For example, when asking yourself how long you want to stay in a trade, you can think about how long you want your capital to be tied up, what indicators you're looking for that will cause you to sell, etc.

When considering how much risk you're willing to take, try a few different scenarios. Also, consider what a profit is to you. Is it a $1 per share a decent profit or do you want to make more? Finally, consider when you want to leave the trade. You should have this written down clearly. Are you going to leave the trade once you've made a certain profit, once you hit the resistance level, or once you see another indication that it's time to go? When you've made your plan, it's important you stick to it. This will help you remain emotionally objective when trading.

Once you've made your exit plan, it's time again to practice. Look at some past charts and analyze where you would have entered and exited the trade, based on the indicators like support and resistance, or based on the moving average. Analyze every piece of a move. Why would a certain exit point have worked or failed? Afterward, try this again with a future chart. You can either do this in a simulation or using your own chart website of choice. Pick a stock you want to follow and find an entry point you think will work for you. Then, using your exit strategy, determine when you will exit the chart. Spend a few days looking at your plan as the chart moves forward. Did your plan work? Are there other ways you could have executed it? Keep practicing, don't just do this with one chart and think you're ready to start trading.

Where to place your stop-loss and why

We've talked a little about stop-losses, but let's look at them in more detail and explore the different types you can use. A stop-loss is very similar to a fire alarm. The fire alarm in your house starts to go off the moment that it senses smoke. It doesn't have to be a literal fire for it to sound the alarm. This can be kind of irritating, but it is also a very close analogy of what a stop-loss is. And yes, on occasion a stop-loss can also be irritating if it's not set correctly. A stop-loss can help you sell your trades when the market turns in an unexpected direction. It's your warning system and safety net in one. It makes sure that if the market is going to drop, you aren't going to lose a massive amount of money. However, sometimes a stop-loss is placed too tight which results in it being triggered during regular market volatility. This is that annoying accidental fire alarm. Even though it can be annoying, a stop-loss can save you considerable grief. As a swing trader, your trades will cover some days and weekends, which can result in precarious nights where the market shifts unexpectedly. A stop-loss can help you ensure your losses aren't too steep.

Chapter 12:

How Purchase of Option Works

To begin options trading, the following are some things to get started with:

1. Initial Preparation

2. Choosing an online broker

3. Finding your options trading niche

4. Finding option trades opportunities

5. Planning individual trades

6. Risk and money management

7. Monitoring your trades

Initial Preparation

It all starts with your mindset. Before you begin options trading, you have to make sure that you have the right mindset of successful options traders. Are you afraid of risk or you are risk lover? What is your attitude towards winning and losing? What is your approach to trading in the financial market? Analyze yourself and see if options trading for you, looking at your deep-seated values.

You also need to develop a trading plan. You've got to develop a trading plan that outlines your entry and exit strategy. If you don't have a long-term plan for options trading, chances are that you will give up in the first three or six months. Have profits targets and income ceiling to hit for options trading.

You also need to develop an action plan to get you doing. You have to make a to-do list for your options trading. How many hours will you be dedicated to the craft and focusing to increase your gains in options trading? How many minutes per day will you dedicate to studying the market and learning about options trading?

Choosing an Online Options Trader

To buy and sell options, you need a verified, licensed, and approved online broker. There is a lot of options broker out there catering for different needs and goals of people. The key is to be clear about your options trading plan and then decided on the type of options broker that will help you to get there. You need to check whether the broker has been approved. You also want to look at the customer service levels of the broker. If you can, call them to ask about brokerage fees, commissions, and service levels. Be clear about what you need so that it makes it easy for you to make your inquiry and find the best online broker that can meet your needs.

The best online brokers are focused on serving their customers. They have the best interest of their customers at heart. Therefore, their services are well-structured to meet their needs and help them to achieve their goals. They also have a high-quality trading platform with tools,

analysis, and guides to help make your options trading fun and exciting.
Finding Your Options Trading Niche

What is your options trading niche? Which kind of trade do you want to focus on? The type of options you choose can be based on your trading plan. Everything flows and revolves around your trading plan. This is why you must invest a considerable amount of time to develop a good trading plan that helps to define your options trading niche. Even if you choose to be a stock options trader, you have to clarify your position. Do you want to be a long-term investor, swing trader, day trader, value investor, or a technical analyst? Would you want to be a net buyer of options or a net seller of options? Usually, a net buyer of options focused on using strategies such as long calls, long straddles, long puts, long strangles and many more.

As a net buyer of options, you play at the debit side of the game, reducing the amount of risk in each trade and increasing your gains. A net seller of options is rather focused on using strategies such as short put, short calls, short straddles, short strangles and much more. In this game, you focus on receiving premiums for placing a trade and capping your risk every trade to maximize gains. You have to choose how to play the options trading and then become an expert in one particular area.

Finding Options Trading Opportunities

Once you have defined your niche, another step is to begin to find opportunities that fit your area of expertise. Finding opportunities have to do with working with your options broker. The main job of your options broker is to know your trading plan and then help you spot opportunities that are in align with your trading plan.

You might also choose to trade in companies that you are comfortable or understand what there are doing. That depends on your trading plan. But to find good options trading opportunities you have to make good use of your trading account and then also dedicate a certain amount of time to study the trade.

Chapter 13:

Covered Call Strategies

N ow that you have your mindset down pat, it is time for you to start understanding the basic strategies of trading options. We will get more into the details of how to trade options using the day trading strategies eventually. For now, let's focus on what it looks like to trade options, including what types of contracts there are and how these contracts are bought and sold.

The first type of option we are going to look at is known as a "covered call." Covered calls are a type of call option that enables you to sell the right to purchase stock to another trader.

You will learn all about what a call option is, in detail, and how it can be sold to others.

What Are Covered Calls?

Call options are a type of options contract that has a buyer whose outlook is bullish and a seller whose outlook is bearish. This means that the individual buying the option believes that the underlying asset is going to increase in value, and the seller believes that the underlying asset is going to decrease in value. Based on this nature, a call option buyer will earn a profit when the underlying asset experiences an increase in price value.

Covered calls are a popular form of call option strategy that is made when the investor only expects a small increase or decrease in the cost of the underlying asset. These particular calls generate income through premiums, which are the prices that people pay in order to purchase the options.

The benefit of a covered call is that the investor gets into the option with the intention of holding a long position with the underlying asset. This way, they experience downside protection while also being able to generate passive income for the individual invested in this particular stock.

The big difference here is that a regular call option is taken for the short term position whereas a covered call option is taken for the long term position. In the end, the covered call provides higher risk protection and greater earning potential.

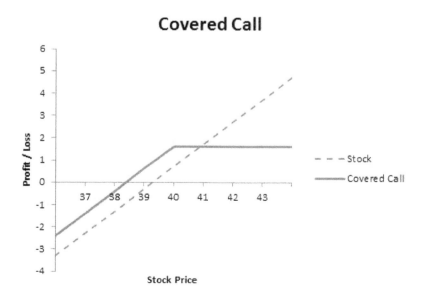

Covered Call Example

Selling covered calls mean that you get paid in exchange for giving up a portion of your future upside. You generally do this as a way to guarantee an increase in your prices, while also creating passive income right away through selling the call option itself.

You engage in covered calls when you think that stock you have already purchased is going to increase in value over a longer period of time. For example, let's say you buy ABC stock for $100 per share, and you believe that it will rise to $120 per share within 12 months. You might create a covered call option that allows people to buy the right to purchase that stock at $110 per share in six months, thus earning you the income from the cost of the contract, known as the premium, right away.

Then, if the buyers of your contract choose to purchase the stock in six months, you also gain the profits from that sale. Although the profits may not be as large had you held the position for the entire six months, they are more guaranteed and reliable than profits in the regular open market.

Writing your covered call takes some practice, but it can earn you a massive amount of profit in the long run. The first thing you need to do is start with identifying what stock you already own in your portfolio that has been performing well and that you are prepared to sell if the call option is assigned to a buyer who wishes to exercise their right to buy.

If you are bullish on a certain stock in the long term, or you believe it is going to increase exponentially, avoid choosing that stock as you may not earn as much profit through the covered call option. Instead, you want to choose a stock that you think is going to increase steadily, but not too incredibly high values so that you do not feel too heartbroken when it is time for you to part with that stock.

After you have chosen your stock you are going to need to choose your strike price, and your expiration date, which will, in turn, create your premium. These are the three elements of the contract that are going to outline how the buying and selling of your stock will work, what level of profit you will gain, and when that particular trade must be executed by in order for it to be valid.

Your strike price is the price that you feel you would be comfortable selling your stock at. When you are writing a covered call, you want to write a strike price that is out of the money or one that is lower than the current value of the stock. This way, should your buyer choose to enact their right to buy your stocks you are earning profits. You want the stock value to increase before you have to sell it to ensure that you are set up to receive profits, otherwise, you may not receive any profits from your trade deal.

The best way to pick your strike price is to look at how the stock has been performing so far, and look at how it is expected to perform going forward. You will want to conduct a technical analysis to ensure that you are following a trend that offers the most likely increase value for your stock prices. This way, when you set the strike price you are remaining reasonable while also creating a profitable price point for yourself.

After you have picked your strike price you need to decide when the option is going to expire. Generally, call options expire within 30-45 days of the call option being created, however, you can certainly increase or decrease that length of time. You are going to want to pick an expiration date that enables you to close out the trade quickly while also having an acceptable premium that people will be willing to pay. If your expiration date turns the premium into too high of a number you will have a difficult time selling your option, or you may never sell it at all.

After you have created your strike price and expiry date, your premium will be automatically determined for your covered call option. Generally, investors will favor premiums that are about 2% of the total stock value as this ensures that they also have the opportunity to make the most off the trade while incurring the least amount of losses.

This means that if you set your expiry date too far out in the future you might increase the cost of your premium too high, preventing investors from wanting to purchase it.

With that being said, always make sure that you are researching what has gone into creating your premium. Sometimes, premiums will seem abnormally high which can occur if there is something going on in the economy that might directly impact the value of the stock that you are trading. If this happens, you might need to adjust your covered call option or choose a different underlying asset to trade. Generally, if something seems too good to be true in the stock market, it is, so beware of premiums that seem too high.

Risks and Benefits of a Covered Call

There are three possible outcomes that you could experience if you were to engage in a covered call sell. The first one would occur if the stock price went down, the second would occur if the stock price stayed the same or slightly increased without reaching the strike price, and the third would occur if the stock rises past the strike price. Each of these outcomes will have different results for you, and you need to be aware of what might happen in each scenario.

Outcome One: The Stock Price Goes Down

If the stock price was to go down at the time of the option expiring, the option would likely expire worthlessly. If the buyer were to exercise their right to buy they would be paying higher than the value of the stock which would not make sense on their behalf. In this case, you would keep the entire premium for selling the contract. The stock price would be down, which may be unfortunate for the rest of your portfolio, but it would be positive that you had profited from the price of the premium.

If this happens, it is important to remember that you are not locked into the position of your contract. The value of the call option you sold will also be decreasing in value, which means that you can buy back the contract for less money than you sold it for so that you are not required to make the sale. Then, you can create a strategy for how you are going to manage the stock you have in your portfolio.

If you think it is going to start moving out of favor you can always dump it, or you can keep it and maintain your position if you think it is still going to behave as you anticipated it would when you bought it in the first place.

Outcome Two: The Stock Stays the Same or Slightly Increases without Reaching the Strike Price

The second scenario is that the stock price barely fluctuates and never reaches the strike price. In this case, there is no bad news. The call option will simply expire worthlessly and you will profit the entire premium from selling it. You may also see some increase in the value of your stock overall, adding a little more profits into your portfolio.

Outcome Three: The Stock Rises past the Strike Price

The third scene occurs when the stock price rises above the strike price, which means the call option is assigned and you will be required to sell 100 stock shares to the buyer.

In this case, you could experience frustration for setting the strike price lower and not receiving the full value of the stock at the point of selling it. While you will still receive profits, they will not be as massive as they could have been which can be frustrating.

Still, you have made profits so there is no reason to fret. You have earned more funds that you can place into your future trades, allowing you to increase your profitability with trading options.

Chapter 14:

Buy a Call

What to Look for to Buy Call Options

When you buy stock, you get what is known as a long position. When you buy a call option you get into a potential long position based on the underlying stock. On the other hand, when you sell a stock short, then you are short selling.

This essentially gives you a short position. Short selling means that you sell at a loss while long selling implies a profit. When you sell a naked call or an uncovered call, you will enter a potentially short position based on the underlying stock.

You enter a potential short position based on the underlying stock when you purchase a put option. Should you sell a naked put, you will enter a potential long position relative to the underlying stock.

If you can understand these four positions and keep them in mind, then you will easily understand the intricacies of selling and buying options. Ideally, you can buy call options and put options as well as sell call options and put options.

Holders: Anyone who buys options is generally referred to as the holder of an option

Writers: A person who sells an option is generally referred to as an options writer

Call and put holders are also known as buyers. They have the right to buy options but are not obligated to do so. They can exercise this right but only within the stipulated time and under the agreed conditions. This way, call and put holders only suffer losses equivalent to the premium charged for the options contract.

Call and put writers are sellers. They have an obligation to sell options or buy should the option expire, and the contract makes money. Therefore, sellers are always expected to oblige to the buyer's wishes. This exposes them to more risks. Therefore, writers stand to lose a lot more than just the cost of writing the options contract.

Example

Think about this company that you really like such that you would like to become a shareholder. According to your predictions, the stock price is going to rise. For instance, the current stock price of this company is $25 but you believe the price will be $35 in a year's time. You can purchase a call option that will grant you the rights to purchase the stock.

On the contract, you can agree to a price of approximately $27 within the succeeding year. This contract will most likely cost you close to $1 per 100 shares. Now if the price does get to $35 as predicted, then you can exercise your right to buy the shares at $27. However, if the price remains constant or falls, you will not be obliged to buy and the only loss you will incur is the options fee.

Basic Put and Call Options Chain

This is a specific chain that is among the most popular options chains used by investors and traders, especially beginners. It is an excellent choice for those seeking to learn more about options.

This chain presents a splittable with put options to the right and call options to the left. The different strike prices relevant to the options run to fight down the center of the table. This way, investors and traders can easily track put and call options of various strike prices. This is demonstrated via the image presented below.

If we closely examine the options chain above, we note that the strike prices run through the middle from top to bottom. We also note that the put options are located on the right side while the call options are on the left-hand side.

Other parameters such as bid price, last price, ask price, volumes, price change from the preceding trading day, and open interested are displayed for both put and call options. When it comes to trading or investing this chain is the most widely used. It is popular with traders basically because it presents a lot of the information, they consider crucial.

Important information necessary to execute trades is presented in a simple manner that is easy to read and understand. Using this chain, a trader can easily trace and identify the available call and put options as well as other parameters affiliated to each option. However, this chain is most suitable for traders interested in simple options trading strategies. There are other chains suitable for more complex strategies.

The Call and Put Options Price

The put and call price is a chain that presents the necessary data relating to basic call and put options. It also projects each option with five option Greeks. This way, an investor or trader who needs to use delta neutral options trading strategies and arbitrage strategies. The trader will be able to effectively make exact calculations regarding size and position to take.

Looking at a relevant chain, you will easily note that all the five Greek symbols that include Vega, Rho, Theta, Gamma, and Delta are used. They are visible in the call and put options price. However, due to challenges in full-screen presentations, options prices usually present as either put options or call options only.

Options Strategies Chains

Specific options strategies chains are ideal for options traders or investors who prefer standardized options strategies like the covered call or the long straddle. The reason is that these chains drastically reduce the amount of work necessary to work out and calculate the options outlay as well as other specifics that relate to the specific strategy.

Options chains like this one generally present only the essential aspects of an options trading strategy across the various expiration dates and strike prices. This way, it can easily calculate and work out the net effect of a position and plenty of other useful detail. This way, a trader can make quick decisions on the spread to choose fast without spending time doing calculations and working out arithmetic.

Call and Put Options Matrix

This chain is the least used by investors and traders, especially beginners and retail options traders. This chain aims to present information on many options including their bid and ask prices over numerous expiration dates all on one page.

This options matrix generally presents only the ask and bid prices for all options listed on the chain but without additional information. This makes it a less useful table especially for beginners, amateurs, and retail traders who basically need a lot more information. However, it is considered by many traders to be the least useful chain out there.

Learn about Options Pricing

Another useful aspect of options trading that you need to be familiar with is the aspect of pricing options. The option price is also known as the option premium and consists of two distinct components. These are the intrinsic value and extrinsic value. Both are governed by the Put-Call Parity principle.

Tips and Tricks When Buying Call Options

• Don't buy a call option with a strike price that you do not think the stock can beat.

• Always include the premium price in your analysis.

• Look for calls that are just in the money. These are likely to bring a modest profit.

• Call options that are out of the money might give you an option for a cheaper premium.

However, the premium should not be your primary consideration when looking to buy a call option. Compared to the money required to buy the shares and the potential profits if the stock goes past the strike price, the premium is going to be a trivial cost in most cases — provided of course the strike price is high enough to take the premium into account.

Look at the time value. If you are looking for larger profits, it is better to aim for longer contracts. Remember, that with any call option you have the option to buy the stock at the strike price at any time between today's date and the deadline when the stock market price exceeds the strike price. Longer time frames mean you increase the chances of that happening. Even if the price goes a little above the strike price and dips down, with a longer window of time before the deadline, you can wait and see if it rebounds. Remember if it never does, you are only out the premium.

Start small. Beginning traders should not bet the farm on options. You will end up broke if you do that. The better approach is to start by investing in one contract at a time and gaining experience as you go.

The best-case scenario for you, as the buyer, is that the stock suddenly starts rising at a high speed before the deadline arrives. You want it to go beyond the strike price so that, when it comes time to exercise your right, you are purchasing your stock at a lower rate than it is now worth. Obviously, you then have the option to instantly list that stock as a covered sell, which would allow you to realize that profit in real money.

That final piece of the puzzle is the important one. As an options trader, you are not in the business of building a stock portfolio. You do not really want to own those shares – you want to make a profit on them as they pass through your hands. You want to buy them for less than they are worth and then sell them on, perhaps even for more than they are worth if you are lucky. It is within that transaction your money will be made.

Buying calls has several advantages for you as an options trader:

It does not cost much to get involved in the movement of a stock. You only need fork out the amount for the premium, after which you can sit back and wait to see what the stock does before making your purchase decision based on actual information, rather than on speculating what the market will do.

It allows you to make use of the kinds of "tips" that market experts have a bad habit of swearing by. You read the news, you are watching the markets and you have information that makes you think a certain stock is about to rise fast and hard. You want to take advantage of that, obviously, and options trading allows you to do so much more safely than simply buying the stock. If you are wrong, you will only lose your premium and you may even make a small profit. If you were wrong and purchased the stock and then it plummeted rather than rose, you stand to lose a whole lot more cash.

Chapter 15:

Buy and Sell Puts

How a Put Option Works?

If you expect the price of a stock to drop, you can profit from this by investing in put options. Put options work in many ways in the same manner as call options. They have an expiration date, they have 100 shares of underlying stock, and their price depends on the price of the underlying stock. Meanwhile, they also suffer from time decay as the expiration date of the option approaches. However, put options actually gain value when the stock price drops, and they lose value when the stock price rises.

This means that put options can be used to "short" the stock. Shorting the stock is just jargon for earning a profit when the stock price declines. Normally, shorting a stock works like this. If you think that a stock is going to drop in value, you borrow shares from your broker — and you immediately sell them on the market at the current stock price. Then, assuming that your bet was the correct one, you buy the shares back when the price drops. Suppose for the sake of example that when you initially borrowed the shares, you sold them at $100 a share. Then the price drops to $80 a share — maybe the company had some bad earnings call, for example. When the price drops, you buy the shares back at $80 a share, and you return them to the broker (remember, you started the process by borrowing shares from the broker). This exercise leaves you with a $20 per share profit.

Of course, most small investors don't have $10,000 or more to chance on schemes like this, but put options enable you to earn profits if the price of a stock declines, using much smaller investments. The idea is basically the same, but when you suspect that the price of a stock is going to drop in the near future, you can buy put options on the stock. A put option has a strike price just like a call option, and when the share price is below the strike price, the put option is in the money. That's because you would be able to buy shares of stock at the market price, and then sell them at the strike price — earning a profit in the process.

Using the same example, we considered before, you could buy a put option with a $100 strike price. Then when the price of the shares dropped to $80, you could buy them on the market, and then sell them to the originator of the put option contract at the strike price - $100 a share. Buying a put option is something that doesn't require a large margin account to do.

When a put option is exercised, that is you sell the stock at the strike price, they say that the stock was "put to" the originator of the option contract. Of course, most options traders are not looking to exercise individual put options. If the stock price were really to drop $20 a share on a stock where you bought put options with a $100 strike price, the value of the put options would go up substantially, because you could exercise them and make solid profits. Since there are other traders who would be interested in selling the stock, you will be able to sell your put option to another trader for a profit. Remember that if you buy to open an options contract, you are not obligated to anything and are free and clear once you sell it to someone else.

Think of put options in the same way as call options, but with the price going up to $100 every time the stock drops by $1. Like call options, the pricing of put options is impacted by many factors, and so this is an ideal relationship that we are thinking about here. But it gives you a rule of thumb to understand how put options works (the more in the money they are, the closer they are going to get to the ideal case). Likewise, if the price of the stock rises by $1, the value of a put option would move down by $100. So, with put options, it's an inverse relationship.

A Put as an Insurance Instrument

You buy put options when you believe the value of a stock is going to decline. If a company has some bad earnings call, this can be a good time to buy a put option. Typically, the price of the stock will drop a lot, possibly over a day or two, and then stabilize at a new, lower level. Any bad news of any kind provides an opportunity to profit from put options. This is a kind of flexibility that doesn't exist for most stock traders and investors, being able to earn money when stocks are declining. The fact that you can open your eyes to the potential that options have in expanding your ability to make profits from the stock market. An options trader has the ability to profit under all possible scenarios of stock market movements.

Chapter 16:

In and Out of the Money

The terms "in the money" and "out of the money" are slang used by options traders to indicate whether an option is really worth something or not. It turns out that even out of the money options are worth something, but before we get to that let's learn what these terms mean and how different call options fit in with the definitions.

The first definition you need to know about is "in the money." A call option is in the money when the strike price of the call option is lower than the current share price. In other words, a call option is in the money when you can buy the shares at a discount price relative to the market price.

To really be worth it, however, you need to understand how the breakeven price fits in. If the stock is trading at $101 a share, technically speaking a call option with a strike price of $100 a share is in the money. However, if you paid $2 per share for that option, then it is not really in the money, because you'd lose $1 a share exercising the option.

So from a practical standpoint, an option has to be positioned such that the market share price has risen enough to account not only for the strike price, but also the price paid to buy the call option. So you need to pay more attention to the breakeven price rather than the in the money price – if you are interested in buying the shares of stock.

Call Options: Out of the Money

So to summarize, a call option is in the money if the share price rises above the strike price. On the other hand, if the strike price is above the share price for a call option, then that option is said to be "out of the money." Out of the money options are less desirable than in the money options, and so they are priced at lower levels. The more in the money a call option, the more the option is worth. However, you should not neglect out of the money options. If an option is a little bit out of the money, but the pricing trend is in its direction, the value of the option can still rise. So you can make profits from out of the money options, although it's a little bit trickier. Holding them overnight can also cause problems because options lose value due to time decay. The key thing to remember about out of the money options is that they expire worthless. That is, if you hold an out of the money option through expiration, once the option expires it has zero value. That means your investment in the option is completely lost. If you are going to trade out of the money options, then you should be sure to get rid of them as soon as possible. This is a good reason to be trading liquid options.

When is an option liquid?

Liquidity is one of the most important concepts in finance and trading. Simply put, liquidity is a measure (vague, but real) of how quickly you can convert something into cash.

A cashier's check is very liquid. Cash is 100% liquid. A bar of gold is pretty liquid because you can take it to a gold or coin dealer and sell it immediately for cash. Stocks are liquid, but less liquid than these items because you can't immediately access the cash you get from selling stocks (most brokers will make you wait a few days).

You can compare liquidity between different types of assets. To explain what we mean, let's focus only on options. Some options are going to be more liquid than others. No matter what, your broker is going to have rules on being able to get the cash out, but that isn't our concern when talking about the liquidity of options. Those rules are going to apply to all options.

Our concern here is how easy it is to buy and sell a particular option.

Options trading can move fast. In my own experience, I have seen options that I've purchased lose and gain $100 or more over a matter of 30-90 minutes. The rapid price movements of options coupled with the fact that they lose value through time decay every single day that passes means that when the time is right to get in and out of an options contract, you want to be able to do it right away.

So the concept of liquidity when it comes to trading options comes down to being able to buy and sell an option instantly. The market provides two important pieces of information that you can use in order to determine how liquid an option is.

Chapter 17:

Market Strategies: 5 Strategies Explained for the Reader

Long Straddle

A straddle is an options trading system that allows traders to have a position in both a put option and a call option with the same exercise price and expiration date. This means that traders have the right to buy and sell a given currency pair at the same exchange rate and for the same period. Traders usually use this system if they do not have a clear view of the future direction of the currency pair in a certain period. However, they are convinced that the currency pair will move significantly.

Long straddle: As the name suggests, a long straddle is simply a strategy in the Forex options trading system, where the trader goes a long (buys) call option and an extended option for the same currency pair at the same exercise price and expiration date.

Rolling Out Options

A rollout is a strategy that is used to extend the lifetime of an option that hasn't quite worked out. This is going to be a strategy used by options sellers. A rollout might be something you would consider doing when you've sold a naked call, and the share price is closing in on your strike price, creating a risk that the option will be exercised. By doing a rollout you can keep the trade going longer, and possibly make some changes to give the trade better odds of being profitable. Typically, you will choose to do a rollout when it is close to the expiration date.

Definition of the Rollout Strategy

A rollout strategy works in the following way. You will close your current option contract by buying it back, and simultaneously open a new contract of the same type, with changes. One way to change is by altering the strike price. Another method that is more common is to move up the expiration date. A common practice is to open the new contract with an expiration date that is further out in the future. For example, you could close a naked put option that is expiring in two days by buying it back and opening a new contract by selling a new naked put option. You would use the same stock and the same strike price, but with an expiration date that is three weeks into the future.

This is a standard strategy where we say that the option contract was rolled out.

You can also follow the same strategy choosing either a higher strike price or a lower strike price. For example, if we have an Apple naked put with a strike price of $205, we could roll up the option by closing this position and selling a new naked put on Apple with a strike price of $206. Alternatively, you could choose a lower strike price. Using the same example, instead of going with a $206 strike price, we could go with a $203 strike price. Maybe, in that case, the Apple share prices are dropping and it got a little too close for comfort. When you select a lower strike price, they say that you have rolled down the trade.

It's also possible to roll out and roll up or down. In other words, you can close your current contract and open a new one that has a further expiration date, but you also change the strike price.

Types of Options Where Rolling Strategies Are Used

You can use a rollout, roll up, or roll down strategy on any type of option, including options that you buy to open (long calls and puts). However, the vast majority of options contracts that are rolled are short (buy to open) options. You can use rolling techniques on any of the major strategies covered here, such as put credit spreads, strangles, or iron condors.

Why Roll an Options Contract

The main reason that options traders roll an option contract is that they are in the money and there is an assignment risk. By rolling it out, you can keep the trade going but avoid assignment. Sometimes just moving the expiration date is good enough to accomplish this. An option can be assigned at any time, but in most cases, it has to reach expiration in order to be assigned. By using a rollout, the trader can avoid this situation. Of course, rolling up or rolling down can also help avoid assignment, since changing the strike price might allow you to move from an in the money situation to an out of the money situation.

There are other reasons that are sometimes used to justify rolling an option. For example, when you are selling for income, you can roll the trade to keep generating more money. Changing market conditions might also be a reason to roll a trade.

When rolling a spread, strangle, or iron condor, there are many possibilities that exist for altering the trade. Suppose you have a put credit spread with strikes of $207 and $204. We could change one or both of the strike prices, and we could also change the expiration date. Maybe we want to tighten or widen the spread, so we could roll out and also roll down the lower strike price, and have a new spread with strike prices of $207 and $202, for example.

A Rollout is a Single Trade

It's important to note that a rollout is one trade, and not two. You are simultaneously closing one option (possibly with multiple legs) and opening a new contract in its place.

Strangle

A strangle is similar to a straddle, but in this case, the strike prices are different. In this case, you will buy a just barely out of the money call option, while simultaneously buying a slightly out of the money put option. The two options will have the same expiry date. The breakeven points for a strangle will be calculated in the same way as the breakeven prices for a straddle, but you will use the individual strike prices for a call and put it because they are different. You calculate the total premium paid, which is the total amount paid for the call option plus the premium paid for the put option. Then the breakeven points are given by the following formulas:

- To the upside, the breakeven point is the strike price of the call plus the total premium paid.

- On the downside, the breakeven point is the strike price of the put minus the total premium paid.

Similar to a long straddle, the maximum loss is going to occur when the share price ends up in between the two strike prices. Therefore, you might want to choose strike prices that are relatively close to minimize the range over which the loss can occur. There is a tradeoff here. The closer in range the strike prices are, the more expensive it is going to be in order to enter the position. But, it's going to increase your probability of profit because if the strike prices are tight about the current share price. There is a higher probability that the share prices are going to exceed the call strike plus the premium paid, or decrease below the put strike price less the price paid to enter the contract (the premium).

Married Puts

Usually, the married puts approach is used when an optional trader is abundant on a stock, wants the benefits of stock ownership (dividends, voting rights, etc.) but wary of short-term uncertainty.

Cash-secured Puts

The term cash-secured put relates to the approach of selling the contract to purchase the security if it is traded at a price below its current market price. Cash-secured putting involves both writing the option and depositing cash into a sweep account to purchase the underlying security.

Chapter 18:

To Become a Successful Trader: Mindset and

Study

No one can guarantee your commercial success. This is a problematic adventure right from the start, and you are up against the brightest. From my own experience as well as from many successful traders, here are five main steps that, if followed earnestly, will put you on the right track for successful trading.

1. Learn How to Read the Chart for Good Trading

Many are looking to sell you the new predictor or device in the trading industry. The statements are always high: not so much of the results, unless proved. You will end up finding it unwise to rely solely on systems and indicators. You get a buying signal that last week was good, but this week, it's not. It occurs very frequently. Why that failed is unclear.

The best thing you can do is learn how to read an uncluttered chart for your trade consisting of price candles and volume. Quantity reveals behind-the-market fuel; the result is the price of that fuel. For instance, if the amount rises after a long rally but the price doesn't rise, it may mean the market has reached a peak. At the very least it shows you that profits are going into the rally. None of the metrics will tell you. Different price and volume trends and trade setups occur in all phases of a business cycle. First, you want to know some time-proven trading metrics of primaries, because they work together when modified and don't conflict with each other. I'm using MACD and RSI as they stood test time and didn't clutter results.

It is important to note that all systems/disciplines need to operate with an excellent trading experience; if you have access to or have established that expertise, then you are off to the races. If not, the ability to disseminate good knowledge from the poor is most important. Understanding these trends will provide you with a real advantage in trade.

2. Practice Sound Money Management Trading

No trading system is 100%. Trades would still lose out. Money management lets you decide how much to lose on each deal, and even with a series of losses, keep you in the game. This will help to identify role sizing and notify the degree of stoppage. Trading success would be elusive without sound money-management practices.

Money management is more than just finding out how much you need to gamble on some specific trade. It also involves items such as when to step upscale. For example, if you are in a trend, you know that this market has a high chance of closing at its peak. This is when sound money management suggests you put the full size of your place on. These times can make a big difference for the week or month in which you profit.

3. Create a Trading Strategy

There's no trading for skilled traders without planning. A trading strategy includes decisions that you will make ahead of time. These include trading markets, trading schedules, timeframes, position sizing, risk parameters, how to make money, how to increase the size of the position, what to do in case of a significant drawdown, when to take advantage of the account and so on.

4. Consider Trading Mental Game

A lot is going on 'between the ears' which affects your trade. Few traders put a great deal of energy into the psychological side of trade before they lose out or find their psychology working against them. They cannot pull the trigger on a sound commercial system, for example. Many professional athletes focus on their game's mental side, as it gives them a competitive advantage. There are two aspects of psychology: one helps you minimize and remove unforced trading errors; the other enables you to improve your trading skills and abilities.

5. Practice Well

This creates unique competences. How can you develop ability without putting it into practice? Simulation and paper-trading for the aspiring trader are highly useful practices. Even traders with experience will always learn new trading concepts. You will learn what trade of preference looks like, the market conditions under which it operates best, the best reasons for entry, and the fair benefit targets from practice trades.

Most of the new traders begin by studying other traders 'trading strategies. Nonetheless, it is easy to build the first trading strategy, but it is hard to develop a sustainable trading strategy.

It's difficult to find an objective trading edge. You'll see the company goes beyond your trading plan successfully. So why should you still be shaping your trading strategy, and why not use a good trader's trading strategy? Traders may be exchanging their resources and approaches, but no trader can guarantee your income or will do so. Every single trader is different. Therefore, you can only benefit from a unique and personal combination of trading instruments. Developing your Trading strategy is the easiest and most sustainable solution.

You will need access to charts to construct a plan that represents the timeframe to be exchanged, an inquisitive and analytical mind, and a pad of paper to list your ideas. You then formalize these concepts into a plan, and on other maps, "visually backtest" them. We are going over the process from start to finish in this article and providing crucial questions to ask along the way. Once you have achieved this, you will be ready to start developing your plans in any market and in any timeframe.

Time & Location

You need to narrow down the chart options before you can build a plan. Are you a day trader, an investor, or a swing businessman? Are you going to trade on a one-minute or monthly timeframe?

Then you want to focus on which market you 're going to trade: stocks, options, futures, forex, or commodities? If you have chosen a timeline and a market, determine what type of trading you want to do. As an example, let's assume that you want to search for stocks on a one-minute timeline for day-to-day trading purposes, and that you want to focus on stocks that move within a range. You can now run a stock screen for stocks that trade within a range and meet certain conditions, such as minimum volume and price criteria.

Assets, of course, change over time, so when appropriate, run new screens to find assets that suit your trading criteria until the former stocks are no longer trading in a manner that suits your strategy.

Creating and Implementing Plans

Having a workable strategy makes it much easier to stick to your business plan because the work is the strategy. Suppose a day trader wants to look at the stocks over five minutes, she has a stock selected for certain requirements from the stock list created by the stock screen she ran. She'll look for money-making opportunities on this 5-minute map.

The investor is going to look at the ups and downs and see if anything has precipitated such movements. All measurements are analyzed, such as time of day, patterns of candlesticks, patterns of charts, mini-cycles, length, and other trends. After a new approach has been discovered, it helps to go back to see if the same thing has happened with other moves on the map. Could this approach have made a profit on the last day, week, or month? If you're trading for more than five minutes, keep looking at just five-minute timeframes, but look back in time and at other stocks that have similar requirements to see if they've done the same.

After you've established a set of rules that would allow you to enter the market and make a profit, look at the same examples and see what the risk will be. To gain income without being interrupted, decide what your stops would need to be on future trades. Analyze price change after entry, and see where a stop should be put on your charts.

You should look for techniques that work over succinct times, depending on how much you choose to look for strategies. Short-term anomalies often occur, which allow you to extract consistent income.

Such tactics may not last longer than several days but are likely to be used again in the future as well.

Keep track of all the tactics you use in a report and include them in a business plan. If circumstances for a specific approach turn undesirable, you can prevent it. You will rely on that in the market when circumstances support a strategy.

Strategies fall in and out of fashion over various periods; changes will sometimes be needed to accommodate the current market and our situation. Build your plan or use somebody else's strategy and check it for a time that suits your choice. You can give yourself some high starting points by looking back to make more money and avoid losses as you get more experience. Track all the techniques you use to be able to use those strategies again when circumstances support them.

Chapter 19:

Trading Psychology

We associate trading psychology to some behaviors and emotions that are often the triggers for catalysts for decisions. The most common emotions that every trader will come across are fear and greed.

Fear

At any given time, fear represents one of the worst kinds of emotions that you can have. Check-in your newspaper one day, and you read about a steep selloff, and the following thing is trying to rack your brain about what to do following even if it isn't the right action at that time.

Many investors think that they know what will happen in the following few days, which makes them have a lot of confidence in the outcome of the trade. This leads to investors getting into the trade at a level that is too high or too low, which in turn makes them react emotionally.

As the trader puts a lot of hope on the single trade, the level of fear tends to increase, and hesitation and caution kick in.

Fear is part of every trader, but skilled traders have the capacity to manage the fear. There are various types of fears that you will experience, let us look at a few of them:

The Fear to Lose

Have you ever entered a trade and all you could think about is losing? The fear of losing makes it hard for you to execute the perfect strategy or enter or exit a strategy at the right time.

As a trader, you know that you need to make timely decisions when the strategy signals you to take one. When you be afraid guiding you, the level of confidence drops, and you don't have the ability to execute the strategy the right way, at the right time. When a strategy fails, you lose trust in your abilities as well as strategy.

When you lose trust in many of the strategies, you end up with analysis paralysis, whereby you don't have the capacity to pull the trigger on any decision that you make. Making a move becomes a huge challenge.

When you cannot pull the trigger, all you can think about is staying away from the pain of losing, while you need to move towards gains.

No trader likes to lose, but it is a fact that even the best traders will make losses once in a while. The key is for them to make more profitable trades that allow them to stay in the game.

The Fear of a Positive Trend Going Negative (and Vice Versa)

Many traders choose to go for quick profits and then leave the losses to run down. Many traders want to convince themselves that they have made some money for the day, so they tend to go for a quick profit so that they have the winning feeling.

So, what should you do instead? You need to stick with the trend. When you notice a trend is starting, it is good to stay with the trend until you have a signal that the trend is about to reverse. It is only then that you exit this position.

To understand this concept, you need to consider the history of the market. History is good at pointing out that times change, and trends can go either way. Remember that no one knows the exact time the trend will start or end; all you need to do is wait upon the signal.

The Fear of Missing Out

For every trade, you have people that doubt the capacity of the trade to go through. After you place the trade, you will be faced with many skeptics that will doubt the whole procedure and leave you wondering whether to exit the strategy or not.

This fear is also characterized by greed — because you aren't working on the premise of making a successful trade rather the fact that the security is rising without you having a piece of the pie.

This fear is usually based on information that there is a trend that you missed that you would have capitalized on.

This fear has a downside — you will forget about any potential risk associated with the trade and instead think that you have the capacity to make a profit because other people benefited from the action.

Fear of Being Wrong

Many traders put too much emphasis on being right that they forget that this is a business they should run the right way. They also forget that being successful is all about knowing the trend and how it affects their engagement.

When you follow the best timing strategy, you create many positive results over a certain time.

The uncanny desire to focus on always being right instead of focusing on making money is a great part of your ego, and to stay on the right path; you need to trade without your ego for once.

If you accommodate a perfectionist mentality when you get into trades, you will be after failure because you will experience a lot of losses as well. Perfectionists don't take losses the right way, and this translates into fear.

Ways to Overcome Fear in Trading

As you can see, it is obvious that fear can lead to losses. So, how can you avoid this fear and become successful?

- Learn

You need to find a way to get knowledge so that you have the basis for making decisions. When you know all there is to know about options, you know what to buy and when to sell, and learn which ones to watch. You are then more comfortable making the right decisions.

- Have Goals

What are your short term and long-term goals? Setting the right goals helps you to overcome fear. When you have goals, you have rules that dictate how you behave, even in times of fear. You also have a timeline for your journey.

- Envision the Bigger Picture

You always need to evaluate your choices at all times and see what you have gained or lost so far for taking some steps. Understanding the mistakes, you made gives you guidance to make better decisions in the future.

- Start Small

Many traders that subscribe to fear have lost a lot before. They put a lot of funds on the line and ended up losing, which in turn made them fear to place other trades. Begin with small sums so that you don't risk too much to put fear in you. Once you get more confident, you can invest larger sums so that you enjoy more profit.

- Use the Right Strategy

Having the right trading strategy makes it easy to execute your trades successfully. Make sure you look at various options trading strategies so that you know which one is ideal for your situation and skills.

Many strategies can help you succeed, but others might leave you confused. If you have a strategy that doesn't give you the returns you desire, then adjust it to suit your needs over time. Refine it till you are comfortable with its performance.

- Go Simple

When you have a strategy that is simple and straightforward, you will be less likely to lose confidence along the way because you know what to expect.

Additionally, the easier the strategy, the faster it will be to spot any issues.

- Don't Hesitate

At times you have to jump into the fray even if you aren't so comfortable with the way it works. Once you begin taking steps, you will learn more about the trade.

However, you need always to be prepared when taking any trade. The more prepared you are, the easier it will be for you to run successful trades.

- Don't Give Up

Things might not always go as you expect them to do. Remember that mistakes are there to give you lessons that will make you a better trader. When you lose, take time to identify the mistake you made and then correct it, then try again.

Greed

This refers to a selfish desire to get more money than you need from a trade. When the desire to get more than you can usually make takes over your decision-making process, you are looking at failure.

Greed is seen to be more detrimental than fear. Yes, fear can make you lose trades, but the good thing is that you get to preserve your capital. On the other hand, greed places you in a situation where you spend your capital faster than you return it. It pushes you to act when you shouldn't be acting at all.

The Danger of Being Greedy

When you are greedy, you end up acting irrationally. Irrational trading behavior can be overtrading, overleveraging, holding onto trades for too long, or chasing different markets.

The more greed you have, the more foolish you act. If you reach a point at which greed takes over from common sense, then you are overdoing it.

When you are greedy, you also end up risking way much more than you can handle and you end up with a loss. You also have unrealistic expectations from the market, which makes it seem as if you are after just money and nothing else.

When you are greedy, you also start trading prematurely without any knowledge of the options trading market.

When you are too greedy, your judgment is clouded, and you won't think about any negative consequences that might result when you make certain decisions.

Many traders that were too greedy ended up giving up after making this mistake in the initial trading phase.

How to Overcome Greed

Like any other endeavor in trading, you need a lot of effort to overcome greed. It might not be easy because we are talking about human emotions here, but it is possible.

First, you have to know that every call you make won't be the right one at all times. There are times when you won't make the right move, and you will end up losing money. At times you will miss the perfect strategy altogether, and you won't move a step ahead.

Secondly, you have to agree that the market is way bigger than you. When you do this, you will accept and make mistakes in the process.

Hope

Hope is what keeps a trading expectation alive when it has reached reversal. Hope is usually factored in the mind of a trader that has placed a huge amount on a trade. Many traders also go for hope when they wish to recoup past losses. These traders are always hopeful that the following trade will be the best, and they end up placing more than they should on the trade.

This type of emotion is dangerous because the market doesn't care at all about your hopes and will take your money.

Regret

This is the feeling of disappointment or sadness over a trade that has been done, especially when it has resulted in a loss.

Focusing too much on missing trade makes the trader not to move forward. After you learn the lessons after such a loss, you need to understand the mistakes you made then move ahead.

When you decide to let regret to rule your thinking, you start chasing markets with the hopes that you will end up making money on a position by doubling the entrance price.

Chapter 20:

Tools and Platforms

You will need to accept the help of some outside 'forces' to succeed in day trading business. Apart from your efforts, three things will decide if you can succeed or not at earning profits from day trading. These are trading platforms, charting software, and brokerage services.

Day trading was made popular by the electronic trading systems, also known as online trading platforms. These are computer software programs, for placing buy and sell orders for different financial products. On online trading platforms, the speed of data feeds and fast execution of orders have made them very popular with day traders. This is one of the reasons why many people now prefer to become individual day traders and conduct their business from any place, especially from their homes.

This is in stark contrast to traditional trading which usually happens on stock exchange floors where brokers yell on telephones and clients find it hard to get their desired trades executed immediately.

Electronic trading platforms also have another advantage. These relay live market prices to the clients' computer screen, which traders can use to decide whether they want to buy, or sell, or hold their positions.

Apart from an online trading platform, day traders also need to have sophisticated trading tools; such as charting software; account management tools; and newsfeed. In today's technology-driven age, one cannot imagine indulging in day trading with no charting software.

This software helps in technical analysis of stock prices, based on which, traders take to buy and sell decisions. Automatic or algorithmic trading is rapidly expanding. Big traders use automatic charting software to generate trading signals that are automatically executed on their behalf.

According to their trading styles, traders have different requirements. Trading software is also based on various trading styles. For day traders, the speed of execution and tools for chart analysis are very important. Brokerage houses provide trading platforms that fulfill these requirements and attract many day traders as their customers. Some other companies have nothing to do with brokerage services but provide standalone charting software of excellent quality.

The third essential requirement for day trading is selecting a good broker, who provides competitive brokerage rates. With every trade, day traders have to pay some fees to the broker, which is called brokerage or commission. Since day traders usually trade in every session and mostly execute more than one trade every day, they need a brokerage plan where the trading commission is at a minimum. Take it this way; as the trading commission, traders incur a financial loss as soon as they place a trade, with every trade. Every trade has two legs; one buys and one sell. The brokerage is charged on both legs. To keep this money-outflow to a minimum, traders need a broker, who provides them necessary day trading facilities but does not charge hefty fees for this.

All these things; online trading platform, charting software, and broker's commission; will also constitute parts of your investment in day trading business. You will need to research and compare various services and tools, before taking a final decision. Once you invest money in these "parts" of the business, it will not be easy to change.

Trading Platforms

Trading platforms are technical tools created with computer software. These platforms are used for trade execution and managing open positions in the stock markets. Online platforms range from a basic screen to sophisticated and complex systems. The simple and basic trading platforms usually provide only order entry facilities, not much beyond that. Advanced trading terminals have many other facilities, such as streaming quotes, newsfeed, and charting facilities.

Day traders should consider their needs while selecting a trading platform. For example, are they at a beginner's level or professional? No need to spend money on highly sophisticated platforms, when you are just beginning your day trading career. Different trading platforms are tailored to suit different markets: such as stocks, forex, commodities, options, and futures.

Based on their features, trading platforms can be divided into categories of commercial platforms and crop platforms. For day traders and retail investors, commercial platforms are more useful. These are easy to use and have many valuable features. On these platforms, day traders will find the news feed and technical charts good for day trading. Investors can use research and education related tools. Prop trading platforms are more sophisticated and are customized for large brokerage houses, who wish to provide a unique trading experience to their clients.

For beginners, it is advisable to go for some basic online trading platform that provides a simple and easy-to-understand interface. In the beginning of the day trading career, it will be difficult to adjust to the market volatility and learn new things with every trade. On top of that, any complicated trading program may confuse a novice day trader and cause losses instead of providing ease of business.

Day traders should consider two factors before choosing a trading platform; its price and available features. A live data feed is a must for any good platform. At the same time, it should not cost the moon and some more. Therefore, the day trader will have to balance between the price and trading features. Going for a cheap platform may help cut costs, but it could provide delayed data which will destroy your day trading business. On the other hand, a fancy trading platform will put a hole in your pocket and confuse you during trading by its overwhelming range of features.

Those, who day trade in options, will need different charting features than those who trade in stocks. Similarly; day traders in forex markets will need different types of trading platforms. Carefully consider what tools are available on any online platform. If that suits your requirements and budget, make a final decision to purchase it.

Some trading platforms are available only for those, who have an account with a broker. Some may have high deposit rates before allowing traders to use it. It is also possible that some online trading platforms will easily give margin facility to their customers; while others may not provide it. All these things should be considered before investing in any trading platform.

Before making a choice, it will be better if you make a list of your requirements, then check that list against the features of any platform. Purchase the one that fulfills all or most of your requirements.

Day Trading Software

Many day traders use computer software for automated trading. This takes away their headache of spotting the trend and deciding the trade entry and exit points. Also, they need not spend hours on chart analysis and reading economic news to understand what will happen in stock markets. Day trading software takes care of all their time consuming and decision-making problems.

These days, trading software automatically analyzes chart signals, decide trade entry and exit points, profit booking and stop-loss levels, and execute the trade on behalf of the trader. The biggest advantage of automated trading is; it takes away the hazards of emotional trading. Not everyone can control their emotions, especially in stock markets, where fear and greed overcome day traders. Under the influence of emotions, they do not spot the right trend and make trading mistakes. This is one of the very common mistakes in day trading, and most of the day traders who suffer losses, do so because they cannot control their emotions.

Different types of automated trading programs are available nowadays. The simplest type of such program is standalone websites that provide trade signals for time-based subscriptions. These websites display trading charts, where real-time prices run through the session and generate intraday buy and sell signals. Day traders have to watch these signals and manually trade on their own trading platform. Such programs cost little, and day traders can continue their subscription, or discontinuous it, based on how much profit they make from it.

Some brokerage firms also provide automated trading programs to their clients. These programs run only on that company's trading platform, and day traders can directly place buy and sell orders from the program.

Choosing a Suitable Broker

In the day trading business, a brokerage service will be like your business partner, which will link you with the stock exchanges and give you a platform to execute your trade. Also, this service will demand a fee from you for every executed trade. Therefore, you will have to consider many points before you choose a broker for day trading.

A high brokerage can create setbacks in your profit-making efforts, and a low brokerage may hide some low-quality features of the trading platform. Since this brokerage service will be the medium through which you will execute your day trading business; compare different services before making your choice.

The first thing to consider will be; does the broker fit your needs? If you are going to focus only on day trading, then you must choose a service where the brokerage will be affordable for you. Check its features whether they are suitable for intraday trading or not. Choosing the right broker will be the first step in investing in your trading business. Investing in the right tools and services will provide a solid foundation for trading.

Different brokers cater to different trading and investing needs. Their tools and features are also tailored according to their customers' needs. A brokerage service, which is focused on long-term investors, may not be a good fit for day traders. In day trading also, there are various services that are tailor-made for day traders of forex markets, some other target day traders in commodities markets. For day trading in stocks, you will have to focus on brokers that have the most comprehensive features for stock traders.

The second most important step in finalizing a broker will be its trading fees and facilities. As a day trader, you will be placing more trades every day. Therefore, a low brokerage will suit your needs. Also, look for margin facilities for intraday traders, which will help you at a fraction of the original cost of trading.

Check out the broker's trading platform. Does it provide a live data feed of markets; or, is there any delay in its price feed? For a day trader, going for a trading platform with a delayed price feed will be like committing hara-kiri. Getting the right price at the right time is a must for making correct trade decisions. Also, the broker's trading platform should have good speed and should not face connectivity problems. Check out social media forums to know what other customers of the broker say about its services.

As a beginner, it will be better to go with a simple brokerage plan that fulfills your basic day trading needs. In the initial stages, you will have to focus on learning how stock markets function, and how to trade correctly. Once you have successfully established your day trading business, and feel confident about various trading tricks, you can think of upgrading your system and go for more advanced trading platforms and charting software.

Remember, tools and services can help you only up to a limit. Your biggest trading accessory will be your knowledge and skills that will help you establish a good day trading business.

Conclusion

ongratulations on reaching the end of this book. It shows real dedication on your part to exploring options day trading as a career for you. In closing, let us quickly recap. An option is a financial contract that facilitates the right to buy or sell an asset by a certain date at a specific price called the expiration date for a certain price called a strike price.

The contract is named an option because the holder of the contract is under no obligation to exercise this right by the date specified. Options are not to be confused with stocks, which are a representation of ownership in an individual company. Stocks are an example of an asset that can be associated with an option.

Options day traders open option positions at the beginning of the day and close them by the end of the day. This is a full-time, challenging career that can be highly lucrative when done right. Benefits of day trading options include:

- Affordability as trading options is significantly lower priced than other major forms of investment like buying stock.
- Having no obligation to buy or sell anything unless it is beneficial to do so.
- Having the ability to build a diverse portfolio.
- Having the ability to gain profit from assets owned.

- Being sustainable.

Call options and put options – these are the two fundamental types of options. Call options give the trader the right to purchase the associated asset on or before the expiry date. Put options gives the trader the right to sell the asset attached to the contract at the strike price on or before the expiry date. These two types of options can further be divided into whether or not the seller owns the associated asset.

How a day trader options chooses to pursue an option position depends on its trading style, and how it performs technical analyzes, refers to price charts and other reference instruments. Trading strategies for the popular options include:

- Covered call strategy
- Credit spreads
- Debit spreads
- Iron condor
- Rolling out options
- Straddle strategy
- Strangle strategy

No matter what strategy or combination of strategies that an options day trader chooses to pursue, it all starts with:

- Practicing proper money management and risk management.
- Ensuring that risks and rewards are balanced.
- Having an effective trading strategy.

- Working with the right brokerage firm for you.

- Having realistic expectations.

- Growing your career over time with practical steps rather than big, moves that are not thought out.

- Ensuring that exits are automated.

- Doing your homework and doing pre-market preparation daily.

- Being flexible, patient, hard-working, and dedicated.

As an options day trader who has found massive success, I recommend this career to anyone who wants a challenge and a job that has no limits.

Don't take on this career out of greed. Love of options trading is necessary for success. You have to love performing trades. You have to love learning techniques and strategies. You have to love keeping abreast as to what is going on, in the financial markets and on the news globally. You have to love technical analysis and reading charts. You have to love applying the power principles. There is much to love about day trading options as long as you are in this for the right reasons.

I wrote this to reach out to the person who has an analytical mind, who has big dreams and is willing to put in the work to make those dreams come true. The knowledge imparted here is a great jump point for your new career. Don't stop here, learn more, read more, watch videos, listen to podcasts, find a mentor, and most importantly; do the work strategically to reap the rewards. Good luck!

Bonus Strategy (Credit Spreads)

Put Credit Spread Basic Setup

The idea of a put credit spread starts with a similar idea that we saw in the case of a debit spread. That is, we are going to be buying and selling two options simultaneously. They are both going to be the same type (in this case put options) and they are going to have the same expiration date. However, they are going to have different strike prices.

The difference between a credit and a debit spread is that this time we are looking to sell an option that has a higher strike price, and hence more valuable. In the case of a debit spread, the goal is to earn money from the stock price declining. In the case of a put credit spread, we are only hoping that the stock price remains above the higher strike price in our spread. We are not going to earn money from the price movement of the stock, this is an income-generating situation. So we don't really care what the stock does other than hoping that it is going to remain above the higher strike price of the two options. So although some people talk about this as being a "bull" credit spread, or a "bet" that the stock price is going to rise, it really isn't either of those things. If the stock price drops some, but it stays above our strike price, we are still going to make money. In fact, all we really care about is that it stays above the breakeven price.

The risk that is associated with a put credit spread is that the stock will drop by a large amount, that turns out to be big enough so that it drops below the upper strike price in the spread. We will look at the risks involved in detail below.

When NOT to sell a put credit spread

There are certain situations that you want to avoid selling a put credit spread. Under normal conditions, selling put credit spreads is a low-risk activity. However, if you are in a situation where the stock is moving by a large amount, with a lot of selloffs, then it is higher risk.

For that reason, you don't want to sell put credit spreads that are going to be active after some earnings call. As we noted on straddles and strangles, an earnings call is one of those times when stock can move by huge amounts. If the stock moves up by a large amount, your put credit spread would be unaffected. If the stock stays about the same or only moves by a small amount, your put credit spread would also be unaffected. But, if the earnings call was negative earnings call that really disappointed investor, the stock price may fall by large amounts — and put your higher strike price put in the money. With that in mind, you want to be conscious of when the earnings call dates are for the companies that you are investing in. And avoid selling put credit spreads during those weeks. Earnings calls are staggered, so when you are on the sidelines with one stock you can be investing in a different stock by selling put credit spreads.

There are other events that can cause your put credit spread to be at risk. A major downturn in the overall market can certainly do so. When the market starts dropping, most stocks are going with it (otherwise the market would not be dropping), and nobody really knows when the stock is going to bottom out. So if this is an ongoing process it might be better to wait on the sidelines or even switch to selling some call credit spreads, which we will discuss below.

However, even in bad markets selling put credit spreads can work. Many very successful traders earned good money continuing to sell put credit spreads (or naked puts as well) during the 2008 financial crisis. The problem with this is you have to be very smart about what you use for your strike prices. Most people will find it easier to switch to selling call credit spreads during these types of situations, including mere "corrections."

Often bad news is hard to predict. At the time of writing, there has been a parade of bad news (as far as the markets are concerned) in the form of what can be described as extrinsic events. That is, these are events that are outside the stock market itself. For example, Trump is involved in his trade war with China. That may or may not be a positive thing, but the markets aren't very happy about it and would like to see a deal worked out. So every time that Trump tweets about raising tariffs, the market goes through a major drop. That could put your positions at risk if you are selling put options. But again, choosing carefully can help avoid too much risk. Also, you can always get out of a position, something that we will be discussing.